Passion Branding

Passion Branding

Harnessing the Power of Emotion to Build Strong Brands

Neill Duffy

with Jo Hooper

www.passion-branding.com

WILEY

Other Wiley Editorial Offices

John Wiley & Sons Inc., 111 River Street, Hoboken, NJ 07030, USA

Jossey-Bass, 989 Market Street, San Francisco, CA 94103-1741, USA

Wiley-VCH Verlag GmbH, Boschstr. 12, D-69469 Weinheim, Germany

John Wiley & Sons Australia Ltd, 33 Park Road, Milton, Queensland 4064, Australia

John Wiley & Sons (Asia) Pte Ltd, 2 Clementi Loop #02-01, Jin Xing Distripark, Singapore 129809

John Wiley & Sons Canada Ltd, 22 Worcester Road, Etobicoke, Ontario, Canada M9W 1L1

Wiley also publishes its books in a variety of electronic formats. Some content that appears in print may
not be available in electronic books.

Library of Congress Cataloging-in-Publication Data

Duffy, Neill.
    Passion branding / Neill Duffy, with Jo Hooper.
        p. cm.
    Includes bibliographical references and index.
        ISBN 0-470-85052-3 (cloth : alk. paper)
    1. Brand name products—Marketing.   2. Brand name products—Case studies.
    I. Hooper, Jo.   II. Title.
        HD69.B7D92 2003
        658.8′27—dc21   2003007458

British Library Cataloguing in Publication Data

A catalogue record for this book is available from the British Library

ISBN 0-470-85052-3

Typeset in 11 on 15 point Goudy by Dobbie Typesetting Ltd., Tavistock, Devon
Printed and bound in Great Britain by TJ International, Ltd., Padstow, Cornwall
This book is printed on acid-free paper responsibly manufactured from sustainable forestry
in which at least two trees are planted for each one used for paper production.

For Marion, Sean and Kyle – my greatest passion in life

Contents

Acknowledgements

As Jo and I have found out over the last twelve months, writing a book of this nature is not an easy undertaking. We have been fortunate to have the help of a number of people around the world who have given of their time and shared their opinions and knowledge with us and this help has been invaluable in shaping much of the thinking expressed in *Passion Branding*.

In particular we would like to thank the many marketers from all corners of the globe whose insights and experiences have added immeasurable depth to *Passion Branding*. For this our thanks and appreciation go to – Adam Morgan, Chuck Fruit at Coca-Cola™, Karl Bistany at Octagon, Iain Banner at Richemont, David Butler at Laureus Sport for Good, Sean O'Neill at Guinness, Michael Brockbank at Unilever and Larry Flannagan at MasterCard™, Sally Hancock at Redmandarin, Bob Heussner at O5, Michael Payne at the International Olympic Committee, Alasdair Ritchie, Ty Speer, Harlan Stone at Velocity, Christopher Weil at Momentum, Ravi Naidoo at Interactive Africa and Stephen Bowey at Old Mutual, Martin Feinstein at Proudly South African and Billy Lascaris at Octagon, and Lisa Murray and the Octagon Marketing team in Connecticut. It is indeed a credit to the marketing community in general and its desire to raise the standards within the industry that these people were all so open to our request to share their knowledge and insights with us. It is also encouraging to note that we were only turned down for one interview from the many we requested and eventually conducted.

We would like to extend our sincere appreciation to all those who provided us with information for the case studies interspersed throughout *Passion Branding*. These contributions are invaluable in bringing the theory contained in Passion Branding to life. Our sincere thanks go to – Juan Carlos Perez at Shell, Phil Tardif and Kelly Brooks at Coca-Cola™, Andrew Sherwood at MTN, Ben Sturner at Lycos, Alex Briggs at Adidas, William Parry and Nicole McGuinness at HSBC, Helen Casey at Old Mutual, Martin Feinstein at Proudly South African, Renata Downing at Maxidor, Denise Lewis and Sue McGregor at Orange, Mr R.S. Cho at Hyundai, Nicky Bowker at Nedbank, Pippa Dunn at NTL, Adriana Justi at Samsung, Jeremy Sampson and Lisa Marsala at Interbrand, Katie Quinton at Flora UK.

As a leading company in the field of sponsorship research, we are grateful to Sports Marketing Surveys for providing us with access to research and statistics which lend credibility to many of the claims made in the book. We would also like to thank Andy Richmond for the research provided by mediaedge:cia. In a similar vein we are grateful for the input from S-Comm Research and from both Jim Taylor and Erica Dreijer at Nota Bene with respect to the *Evalu8* sponsorship evaluation tool.

We are also indebted to many of our Octagon colleagues around the world who have assisted in giving us access to and information concerning the major sponsors in their respective territories, have shared their thoughts with us and challenged our thinking. For this we are particularly grateful to Karl Bistany, Phil de Picciotto, Aidan Day, Lance Hill, Lisa Murray, Mariso D'Amico, Woody Thompson, Sean Downes, Fulvio Danilas, Jeff Ehrenkrantz, Beth Parker, Sally Dean, Ros Ryder and Joy Campbell. To the team at Octagon South Africa, a very big thank you. They provided a 'test bed' for a lot of the thinking that sits behind *Passion Branding* and are, in our opinion, leading the way in terms of how Passion Branding is being positioned as a major piece of the marketing mix in South Africa.

Several other people also deserve special mention for their worthwhile assistance in various ways – Sally Hancock and Simon Robinson for providing many useful contact names and suggestions for case study material; Chris Couchman at Coca-Cola™ for his introductions; Lauren Cousins for researching case study information and Gail Rayner for tirelessly transcribing the hundreds and hundreds of pages of copy from the various Thought Leader interviews.

Neill Duffy & Jo Hooper

A big thank you to my wife Marion and very understanding children Sean and Kyle for your patience, understanding, support and love during all the hours that you had to spend without me whilst I was locked up in my study... and Marion, thank you for all the cups of coffee and the snacks and the encouragement that kept me going when I would rather have been outside enjoying beautiful Cape Town with you. To Jo Hooper – I couldn't have done it without you. Your commitment to tracking down the very best case studies around has been, as usual, a source of inspiration – thank you.

Neill Duffy

1

Passion branding – a
new way of marketing

'Passion branding: a relationship between a brand and its consumers around a consumer passion, and the leverage of that passion in order to create stakeholder value'

In a world of switched-off and disenchanted consumers, the time is right for a new way of communicating with these consumers, one which is grounded in a deep appreciation of the *people* that purchase and use our brands, their likes and dislikes, concerns and needs, hopes and aspirations, passions and interests; a new way in which marketers focus on the needs of the *people* that use their brands as much, if not more than, on the needs of the businesses that own those brands; a new way where marketers gain permission from *people* to talk to them rather than simply interrupt whatever it is that they might be doing in the hope of catching their attention; and a new way where *people* feel that they can trust, respect and have a relationship with the brands that they let into their lives.

Most marketers have over the years used sponsorship or cause related marketing to some degree as part of their communications mix. From my perspective however, the majority of marketers have not used these marketing disciplines as effectively as they could have done.

In a changing world, which I have labelled the 'Passion Economy' and which I introduce in Chapter 2, the traditional marketing model is no longer appropriate. I believe that the time is now right for a new way of marketing, a way centred on a relationship between a brand and its consumers, around a consumer passion, and the leverage of that passion in order to create value for all involved in the relationship; a new way of marketing which I call 'passion branding'.

Passion branding, if managed effectively, has the unique ability to multi-task in delivering against a range of business, marketing and communications objectives, a feature not evident in any other single form of communication. Passion branding's role as a brand builder is covered in detail in Chapter 3 while Chapter 4 covers the many other areas in which this versatile business tool can play a role. The amazing thing is that passion branding is one of the few business tools that has the ability to positively impact on all stakeholders in a business relationship and play a major role in helping a business to make a real difference in the lives of people while making a profit for its shareholders.

Right from the outset it is important to appreciate when reading this book that passion branding is not just sponsorship – it is so much more than that. Passion branding is about harnessing the power of people's passion to build strong brands and drive the bottom line. In Chapter 5 therefore I explore the various platforms available to a passion brander, from sponsorship to cause related marketing, from social responsibility marketing to public/private sector partnerships and what I call public domain sponsorships.

Following an understanding of the *why*, Chapter 6 moves into the details as to *how* effective passion branding campaigns should be approached and managed. I provide a passion branding road map which passion branders can use to guide them through the process of identifying the role that passion branding can play in their business and how best to leverage maximum results from the passion branding initiatives.

The greatest challenge facing the passion branding industry is that of measurement. Despite the huge benefits that the discipline offers no generally accepted measurement practice exists and, given the nature of passion branding, I do not believe that it ever will. Measurement around this genre of marketing will continue to be an art rather than a science. Chapter 7 explores the issue of measurement in depth and provides guidelines that passion branders can use to both justify their investment in this area as well as help focus their efforts on those aspects of passion branding that will have the greatest effect on their brands and bottom lines.

As with every industry there are challenges that need to be addressed. Chapter 8 explores some of these and provides a starting point for debate amongst passion branders as to how these should be best overcome.

In each chapter of *Passion Branding* you will find best practice case studies drawn from around the world. They all make for wonderful reading and provide hard support for the various opportunities that passion branding presents. Equally valuable are the thoughts of a group of practitioners within the industry that I consider to be leading the way in terms of how passion branding is evolving as a serious marketing discipline. Drawn from all sides of the industry – client, agency and property owners – they provide invaluable insights that we can all learn from.

I hope you enjoy *Passion Branding* as much as I have enjoyed writing it. My hope is that you will use the book as a constant reference guide and in its pages find some direction as to how to maximize the return that you, your passion partners and your shareholders gain from this extraordinary business tool.

2

The Passion Economy –
a new way of thinking

Where we've come from ... and where we've got to

The relationship between consumers and business has, over the last century, come full circle with the balance of power now having shifted firmly back into the hands of the consumer.

Despite all the technological advances witnessed over the last 100 years such as those in IT, medicine, electronics, space travel and the like, the relationship between consumers and business has, in many respects, started reverting back to that evident over a 100 years ago, that is a relatively personal one where the shopkeeper talked to his customers, knew their names and habits and pretty well understood their needs and wants, likes and dislikes.

The one major difference of course is the scale on which things now happen in terms of the number of consumers participating, the number of products and services on offer and of course the geography involved.

Brands have moved to centre stage as a commonplace way to try and differentiate what have become otherwise commodotized products and services. Everyone is trying to build a brand.

Add to this the fragmentation of mass media – once the mainstay of traditional marketers wanting to reach millions of consumers with their messages in a cost-effective manner – and you quickly realize that it is a complex new environment in which marketers now need to operate.

The passion economy – new trends and expectations

With the benefit of hindsight, and with some fresh insights into where consumers' heads and hearts are currently at, there are a number of trends that point towards the emergence of a new economy, which I have termed the 'Passion Economy'.

This is an economy where brands on their own are no longer enough, where consumers demand that they be treated like people and that marketers respond to both their customers' emotional and their functional needs.

Let us take a look at these trends and how they are shaping the passion economy.

Product to experience – a new offering

Whilst consumers may have historically purchased products, people now want to immerse themselves in positive experiences that address their needs, concerns, hopes and aspirations – perhaps in response to a need to escape from the realities of their day-to-day lives.

Companies marketing products to people therefore need to provide brand experiences that go way beyond the functional attributes of those products and enhance the experience enjoyed by the people consuming their products. Consumers are no longer satisfied with just buying a pair of running shoes – they want to be entertained and enjoy themselves while they do it.

Starbucks provide a wonderful example of this. Thanks to their efforts, over the last decade in their major markets they have transformed coffee from a simple product to a lifestyle experience and in the process have raised the bar in terms of how much people are now prepared to pay for a cup of coffee served alongside the right experience. Their success is based on an insight into what it is that their customers are after; no longer a simple cup of coffee but rather a lifestyle experience with coffee as one of the main actors. The premium price that consumers are prepared to pay for a cup of Starbucks' coffee as compared to the average cup of coffee is directly attributable to the value-added experience that consumers feel they receive from Starbucks.

This is the age of experiential marketing, where experiences exist as a fourth economic offering alongside commodities, goods and services played out in response to people's desires to be feted in a personal and memorable way.[1]

Company to consumer – customers in charge

As was highlighted earlier in this chapter, the balance of power has shifted away from the company and into the hands of the consumer. As a result, consumer activism is now a real factor that companies need to contend with. In some extreme cases consumers are organizing themselves to bring about change in companies that demonstrate undesirable business practices – and succeeding.[2]

The *Cluetrain Manifesto*,[3] written by IT savvy consumers throughout the world, reinforces the web-enabled changes that have taken place in recent years, firstly in respect of the relationship between consumers and companies and secondly in respect of the influence that consumers now have over brands and companies in general. 'We are not seats or eyeballs or

---

[1] B. Joseph Pine II and James H. Gilmore, *The Experience Economy: Work is Theatre & Every Business a Stage* (Boston: Harvard Business School Press, 1999). This is a wonderful book for those wanting to gain further insight into experiential marketing and is strongly recommended reading for passion branders.

[2] Naomi Klein, *No Logo* (London, Flamingo, 2001). This visionary manifesto provides great insight into how modern day consumers view modern day brands and more importantly how they are responding to branding as a whole. Again, a must read for passion branders wanting to better understand the environment in which they are operating.

[3] www.cluetrainmanifesto.com. Read it, it's free.

end-users or consumers, we are human beings – and our reach exceeds your grasp. Deal with it', say its authors.

Of the 95 theses included in the manifesto, there are a couple which really drive home the changing attitude of consumers towards business and the consequent rise of the consumer:

'88. *We have better things to do than worry about whether you'll change in time to get our business. Business is only a part of our lives. It seems to be all of yours. Think about it, who needs whom?'*

'89. *We have real power and we know it. If you don't quite see the light, some other outfit will come along that's more attentive, more interesting, more fun to play with.'*

Share of wallet to share of consumer – the whole person

In most categories, the functional attributes of a product alone no longer drive consumer purchasing behaviour. In a world of product parity where technological innovation is copied at the drop of a hat, the 'soft' issues are the area in which consumer loyalty can be won or lost by brands.

A company's response to these 'soft' issues encompasses all those things that a company or brand does in the community in which it operates and sends out a message about the company's or brand's attitude towards doing business and the people with whom it does business.

In response to this insight, Unilever, by way of example, has taken the decision to break with tradition in the FMCG category and move from a very product-based to a value-based system of communication as Unilever's Michael Brockbank explains:

Leading Thought
Michael Brockbank, *Vice President Brand Communication, Unilever*

We've learned that in today's environment it's impossible to continue to rely on functional points of difference. Rather, we need to depend on communicating and connecting with the consumer using a set of values which they find very attractive and that's actually a lot more difficult to handle than the functional approach.

The second challenge we face is to identify how to engage the consumer such that they want to hear our message. We need to reward them so that they feel it's beneficial to them to listen to us as well as being beneficial to us.

With regards to our value-based approach, we're trying to place our brands in a much broader context of the consumer's lives. So in trying to gain consumer insight, we're investing in understanding what's in the hearts and the stomachs of our consumers as it were, rather than just peering into their brains.

So we look for opportunities where our brands can play a greater role in peoples' lives and if they can, people might then feel strongly about their choice for our brand. You can generally say that there aren't many of our brands which consumers feel passionate about. So we look for areas of activity, relevant to our consumers that they do feel passionate about and try to share their passion in a relevant way. If we can connect it with things they feel passionate about rather than just interested in, then that's a much more valuable relationship.

A fantastic example of this approach is the laundry detergent campaign which started off in Brazil and has moved around the world. After many years of us saying that stains were dirty, we placed stains on children's clothes as an essential part of growing up. If kids are dirty they're dirty: they can't be creative and develop their skills without getting dirty. So accept the fact that they're going to get dirty and just take it for granted from us that it's not an issue with our brand because the stains are going to go anyway. That's an example of putting a brand, a fairly functional brand, in a much broader context to people's attitude towards life.

We are also trying to find new points of engagement with our consumers. In traditional media like television, that means making sure that our contents are more engaging. But it's more than that: it's about finding ground through PR, through editorial, through sponsorship activities, through internet sites and through consumer relationship marketing. It's about engaging with them more when they want to engage with us rather than when we want to engage with them and that's the area of course in which sponsorship is playing an increasing role.

It would therefore seem appropriate that in the passion economy, marketers need to focus on gaining 'share of person' as opposed to 'share of wallet' as well as considering how best to embrace the hearts, minds and souls of the consumers that they are marketing their products and services to. Those companies and brands that get it right will be able to develop a degree of loyalty between themselves and their consumers not seen before which will translate into profits and long-term value.

Short-term gains to long-term value

The last two decades have seen the reporting periods of companies shrink from the traditional annual assessment to a situation where a company's share price, and its executives, almost literally live or die on the company's quarterly results.

Investment analysts now influence the behaviour of corporate executives to such an extent that manipulating the numbers for the sake of achieving their targets appears to be becoming more and more prevalent amongst CEOs. This model is not sustainable and the proverbial 'bubble' has begun to burst as recent examples in the United States – Enron, Worldcom and many others – have shown.

While profits will always be important, shareholders are currently reassessing their focus on short-term gains in favour of the creation of long-term value. This shift in focus is in turn resulting in a reassessment of how best companies should manage their relationships with their customers with life-time value of customers taking precedence over short-term sales and the importance of brand equity moving to the fore like never before.

Consumers – receptive to sceptical

Consumers are becoming very marketing savvy. They now, more so than ever before, understand the motivations behind marketing.

Up until now, this 'education' of consumers has essentially been a passive or a natural development with consumers arriving at their own conclusions based on their own experiences and what they have seen happening around them. However, a recent development in Britain may just accelerate this process. The National Consumer Council has recently introduced a new feature to the 'citizenship' module of the school curriculum in Britain in terms of which children will learn about the power branded goods hold over society and be taught how to resist the pressure to buy them and, it is hoped, made more cynical about the images they see on television.[4]

Little trust in corporates and CEOs

Time magazine has labelled the current period in the US as the 'Season of Mistrust'. A June 2002 *Time*/CNN poll conducted after a number of accounting scandals in the US indicates that 59 per cent of Americans have less trust in major American corporations now than before the scandals; 71 per cent think that the typical CEO is less honest and ethical compared with the average person; and 72 per cent believe that the accounting scandals are indicative of a pattern of deception on the part of a large number of companies.

Even more astounding is the statistic from the same poll that shows that over 57 per cent of Americans rate the moral and ethical standards of CEOs, stockbrokers, the news media, religious leaders and accountants as poor or fair.

The Economist highlights the most vivid example of this fall from grace – General Electric's former CEO Jack Welch. Following on from the corporate failures at Enron and Andersen, GE has also come under the spotlight as Americans turn against their former hero once described by the publication as 'the most successful manager of the past quarter century'.

The sobering reality of all of this is that the American view is not materially different in the rest of the developed world. Europe too has had its share of corporate failures attributed to previously 'revered' CEOs.

The loss in faith in the corporate world has had a devastating effect on consumer confidence and the relationship between brands and consumers seems destined to be a rocky one for brands that do not go out of their

---

[4] Victoria Fletcher, Children will learn to resist the power of big branding (*Evening Standard*, Monday 4 November, 2000).

way to demonstrate their bona fides in a relevant and meaningful way.

11th September – back to basics

Probably one of the defining moments of current history is the September 11 attacks on the World Trade Center in New York and the Pentagon in Washington in 2001, which changed the world, as we knew it. The events of September 11 have forced many people around the world to re-evaluate their priorities in life, their values and their outlook generally. As a result, people are now also taking a harder, closer look at the companies that they support and do business with or work for.

The 2001 Cone/Roper Corporate Citizenship Study, conducted nationally in the US before and after September 11, identifies a major shift in Americans' attitudes towards the role that companies should play in society. In the wake of September 11, and despite an economic downturn, more Americans than ever are demanding that companies play an active role in supporting social needs and are increasingly making purchasing, employment and investment decisions to reward companies that do.

According to Carol Cone, CEO of Cone, a Boston-based strategy firm that links companies and social issues, 'We are seeing extraordinary jumps of 20 to 50 per cent in public opinion since September 11 which accelerated and intensified a trend that we have documented since 1993. Corporate citizenship should now become a critical component of business planning as Americans are promising increased support for companies that share their values and take action'.

So September 11 would seem to have fast-tracked a trend that sees consumers' expectations of corporate America extending beyond the provision of functional benefits to something a lot deeper. This trend is not restricted to America with a similar mood prevalent and well-documented in various studies conducted in Europe, Australia and South Africa.

Key Insights into the passion economy

As we enter the 21st century, the reality is that the world is a different place to that which brand marketers have operated in over the last century. As a result, the effectiveness of the 'tried and tested' mass-marketing approach should now be questioned as a new marketing paradigm is screaming out for attention, one that is centred around a real empathy for the people that consume our brands.

In summary, the passion economy differs from the old economy in the following ways:

The Old Economy		The Passion Economy
Business in charge	⇒	Consumers in charge
Product/Service offering	⇒	Experience offering
Short-term gains	⇒	Long-term value
Share of wallet	⇒	Share of person
Receptive consumers	⇒	Sceptical consumers
Materialism	⇒	Return to basic values

Leading Thought
Ravi Naidoo, *Managing Director, Interactive Africa*

Marketing is facing a huge challenge. It is a crisis of authenticity. The more you look at some of the campaigns leveraged by marketers, the more they look the same. We seem to live in an age of super parity – similar products being overlaid by similar marketing campaigns. Most marketers have access to like resources – consultants, PR companies, spin doctors, ad agencies, custom publishers *et al.* And this machinery is mostly churning out vanilla!

There is a new orthodoxy...more of the same, more banal, more commonplace. For example, magazine titles are proliferating but so many look like reasonable facsimiles of each other – formulaic titles under license of sameness. Marketing clones...metastasizing at a rate of knots.

The biggest tragedy is the aloofness and distance of most of the communication. It is marketing, once removed. Marketers seem to be technicians merely tinkering with the apparatus. These marketers are more method actors than passion players. They obsess about technique rather than thought, mostly placing science over art. They need to use their native intelligence. And they really must go out more naked, whenever possible.

Besides, there seems to be orthodoxy of speech (Do all these marketers go to the same cram college?!) With the pervasive reach of media, most marketers read the same articles and start to sound alike. Welcome to the world of cut-and-paste marketing, delivered with disembodied voices via the ubiquitous Powerpoint presentation. They quote Drucker, Peters, Porter...or that last article in *Fortune*. But how many are really creating something new?

Quite frankly, it needs a blood rinse. It needs to be more human, more visceral, more authentic. We need to reclaim our ability to speak in a language that is candid, frank and honest. The winning marketers are those who will engage in a discourse with their customers in a wholesome repartee that is beyond spin, hype and hoopla!

Marketing needs to rediscover its art.

Harley Davidson are trailblazers in the art of creating a cult phenomenon – they spend less that $500,000 on advertising but the almost-primal connection they share with Harley aficionados is legend. From Sunday morning rides to lifestyle-oriented merchandise, Harley Davidson understands that relationships are the new media.

We really need to tell more stories. We need to laugh more, and take ourselves less seriously. We need to create a unique mythology. Customers are not targets or LSMs.[5] They have lives, in which the marketer's products and services do not rank too highly in their hierarchy of needs. We need to take them seriously.

With the advent of CRM[6] and other arcane TLAs (three-letter acronyms), the challenge is to be hi-tech yet hi-touch. To ensure that the customer relationship is respected, we require hi-fidelity. People need to be engaged and allowed the opportunity to interact with the market; no longer the clarion call of His Master's Voice broadcast in a unilateral manner. In fact, in the words of those good guys at Cluetrain, 'good marketing is really about great conversation.'

---

[5] LSM is an acronym used in South Africa and refers to Living Standard Measure. The population is segmented into LSM groupings from 1–10 based on the socio-economic status of a group (1 being the least status and 10 being the highest status). It is based on 29 household variables – things such as ownership of, or access to, the following are used to determine one's LSM grouping – hot running water, microwave oven, TV set, home telephone, type of dwelling, electricity, motor vehicle in household, home security service etc.

[6] Customer relationship management.

I love the phenomenology experiments of a decade ago such as Adidas apparel being picked up by 'rave bunnies' in clubs in Europe and Hush Puppies by New York hipsters.[7] In both instances, these mature brands were revitalized, despite the best efforts of their ad agencies and marketers. They became cult phenomena as they diffused from their points of origin courtesy of the trendsetters. The effect was swift and better than money could buy. The people decided. It was a classic case of market pull.

People are searching for authenticity. In a perverse way, the public's newfound obsession with Reality TV is a demonstration of this need! Show me the real thing! Sod your GM-enhanced offerings, we want ours organic!

Agreed. The idea needs to be celebrated. Ideas are the enduring, indestructible assets. Like the natural law of energy, ideas can never be destroyed, only transformed. But even the idea, without empathy and understanding of people, is meaningless.

The only complexity in marketing is understanding people. Even now, in the 21st century, this is elusive. Marketers must understand that the difficulty is not in software programmes, spreadsheets, financial modelling or research surveys. It's in the struggle to be a person.

Passion branding – building relationships in the passion economy

Armed with the insights into the passion economy gleaned from the first part of this chapter, let us now take a look at some of the rules of engagement for marketers wishing to build relationships with consumers through a passion branding initiative.

---

[7] In the mid-1990s sales of Hush Puppies were considerably down and the manufacturers were actually thinking of taking the brand off the market. However, quite by chance, Hush Puppies executives learnt from a New York stylist that their brand of shoe had become a trendy item in the clubs and bars of Manhattan. Suddenly designers across America were wanting to use the shoes in their fashion shows and the brand underwent a complete revival all thanks to consumer influence and not additional marketing spend. It represented an anti-establishment protest with kids choosing to wear the shoes because no one else found them fashionable, fashion designers picking up on it to show that they were in touch with the latest trends and then people who followed the fashions set by designers deciding Hush Puppies must be in fashion and so starting to wear them.

Striking a chord with disenchanted customers

The winners in the passion economy will be those companies and brands that understand the way that consumers now view the world and the role that they expect responsible companies and brands to play in that world.

This is suitably summarized in certain theses of the *Cluetrain Manifesto*[8] which provide some useful insight into the opportunity that exists for brands to develop a relationship with consumers in the passion economy.

1. Markets are conversations.
2. Markets consist of human beings, not demographic sectors.
3. Conversations among human beings *sound* human. They are conducted in a human voice.
23. Companies attempting to 'position' themselves need to take a position. Optimally, it should relate to something their market actually cares about.
34. To speak with a human voice, companies must share the concerns of their communities.
35. But first, they must belong to a community.
36. Companies must ask themselves where their corporate cultures end.
37. If their cultures end before the community begins, they will have no market.
80. Don't worry, you can still make money. That is, as long as it's not the only thing on your mind.

Understanding what matters to consumers . . . sorry, people

More so than ever before, marketers need to understand what matters most to the people that buy their brands.

Too often, marketing decisions are taken based on simple demographic research without enough consideration given to what people are passionate

---

[8] www.cluetrainmanifesto.com

about, what drives them, what they are concerned about, their needs, wants and aspirations, how they consume their passions and what role they expect brands to play in the relationship that they have with their passions.

Earning their respect

As consumers become increasingly sceptical towards the marketing efforts of companies and brands, marketers should be looking for an opportunity to demonstrate to those same consumers that a company or brand can have the best interests of its consumers at heart whilst not losing sight of why it is in business in the first place.

This is however a process that requires that companies and brands earn the respect and trust of consumers by demonstrating their bona fides, by putting as much back into the lives of those consumers as they take out for their own benefit. It has become a two-way thing.

At the heart of earning this respect is the marketer's commitment to really doing good and making a positive and genuine contribution towards the consumer community that it has elected to support. The most successful campaigns are those that include a range of activities from support for the élite activities all the way down to the grass roots development of the platform itself.

Conversely, a company or brand which simply 'badges' an activity or lifestyle (for example, by simply sponsoring the broadcast of an event, without contributing anything to the development of the activity itself or the fan experience around the activity) will find themselves enjoying short-term gains in awareness for their businesses or brands at the expense of an eroded brand equity. Consumers will see through these initiatives and label the companies or brands involved in such activities as 'takers, not givers' with potentially negative implications for the company or brand.

South Africa provides some interesting insight in this regard as the socio-political environment in the country after independence in 1994, required that as much focus be paid by brands on the development and reconstruction of South African society as on the visible 'élite' or 'developed' end of the various areas that they supported.

I will not attempt here to debate the effectiveness of the development initiatives themselves; suffice to say that just about every major sponsorship campaign undertaken in South Africa over the last eight years has included a development component. Research conducted during this period confirms that South African consumers, particularly those previously disadvantaged by apartheid, regard such sponsoring companies and brands as caring companies, a much sought after brand attribute in the context of the 'new South Africa'.

There is a lesson in all of this to be learned from the South African experience by marketers operating in the developed world. Passion branding campaigns that address the needs of fans at every level are much more effective than those that simply address a single element of fan needs.

3

Building brands in the passion economy

The value in brands, or brand equity as branding guru David Aaker[1] refers to it, can be attributed to a myriad of different factors ranging from a brand's associations to its customers' loyalty and its perceived quality to the awareness that it enjoys.

Although the consumer landscape may be changing, the traditional view on the role that brands play in any company's business model still seems to hold true amongst industry professionals. Brands continue to provide consumers with a degree of confidence *vis-à-vis* product quality and/or service which in the process simplifies their buying process. As the number of choices within any given category explodes, so too will the importance of familiar brands. Brands are here to stay and are more important than ever before.

Think about this for a moment. According to the Brand Name Educational Foundation,[2] the educational arm of the International Trademark Association, the number of brands in grocery stores worldwide has, over the last ten years, climbed threefold to 45,000.[3] And this is just in the grocery store. Think about the extent to which the number of brand names has increased in other categories, from motor vehicles to financial services institutions.

---

[1] David A. Aaker & Eric Joachimsthaler, *Brand Leadership* (New York: The Free Press: 2000). Aaker has written some excellent stuff on brand management all of which should be compulsory reading for serious passion branders.

[2] www.bnef.org

[3] msnbc.com, August 2002.

Table 3.1 The world's most valuable brands as seen in *BusinessWeek* on 5 August, 2002. Reprinted with permission from Interbrand

2002 Ranking	Brand	2002 Brand Value ($MM)	2001 Brand Value ($MM)	% change, 2001–2002	Country of Owner-ship
1	Coca-Cola	69,637	68,945	1%	US
2	Microsoft	64,091	65,068	−2%	US
3	IBM	51,188	52,752	−3%	US
4	GE	41,311	42,396	−3%	US
5	Intel	30,861	34,665	−11%	US
6	Nokia	29,970	35,035	−14%	Finland
7	Disney	29,256	32,591	−10%	US
8	McDonald's	26,375	25,289	4%	US
9	Marlboro	24,151	22,053	10%	US
10	Mercedes	21,010	21,728	−3%	Germany
11	Ford	20,403	30,092	−32%	US
12	Toyota	19,448	18,578	5%	Japan
13	Citibank	18,066	19,005	−5%	US
14	Hewlett-Packard	16,776	17,983	−7%	US
15	American Express	16,287	16,919	−4%	US
16	Cisco	16,222	17,209	−6%	US
17	AT&T	16,059	22,828	−30%	US
18	Honda	15,064	14,638	3%	Japan
19	Gillette	14,959	15,298	−2%	US
20	BMW	14,425	13,858	4%	Germany
21	Sony	13,899	15,005	−7%	Japan
22	Nescafe	12,843	13,250	−3%	Switzerland
23	Oracle	11,510	12,224	−6%	US
24	Budweiser	11,349	10,838	5%	US

Table 3.1 (continued)

2002 Ranking	Brand	2002 Brand Value ($MM)	2001 Brand Value ($MM)	% change, 2001-2002	Country of Ownership
25	Merrill Lynch	11,230	15,015	−25%	US
26	Morgan Stanley	11,205	N/A	N/A	US
27	Compaq	9,803	12,354	−21%	US
28	Pfizer	9,770	8,951	9%	US
29	JP Morgan	9,693	N/A	N/A	US
30	Kodak	9,671	10,801	−10%	US
31	Dell	9,237	8,269	12%	US
32	Nintendo	9,219	9,460	−3%	Japan
33	Merck	9,138	9,672	−6%	US
34	Samsung	8,310	6,374	30%	S. Korea
35	Nike	7,724	7,589	2%	US
36	Gap	7,406	8,746	−15%	US
37	Heinz	7,347	7,062	4%	US
38	Volkswagen	7,209	7,338	−2%	Germany
39	Goldman Sachs	7,194	7,862	−9%	US
40	Kellogg's	7,191	7,005	3%	US
41	Louis Vuitton	7,054	7,053	0%	France
42	SAP	6,775	6,307	7%	Germany
43	Canon	6,721	6,580	2%	Japan
44	IKEA	6,545	6,005	9%	Sweden
45	Pepsi	6,394	6,214	3%	US
46	Harley Davidson	6,266	5,532	13%	US
47	MTV	6,078	6,599	−8%	US
48	Pizza Hut	6,046	5,978	1%	US
49	KFC	5,346	5,261	2%	US

(continued)

Table 3.1 (continued)

2002 Ranking	Brand	2002 Brand Value ($MM)	2001 Brand Value ($MM)	% change, 2001–2002	Country of Ownership
50	Apple	5,316	5,464	−3%	US
51	Xerox	5,308	6,019	−12%	US
52	Gucci	5,304	5,363	−1%	Italy
53	Accenture	5,182	N/A	N/A	US
54	L'Oreal	5,079	N/A	N/A	France
55	Kleenex	5,039	5,085	−1%	US
56	Sun	4,773	5,149	−7%	US
57	Wrigley's	4,747	4,530	5%	US
58	Reuters	4,611	5,236	−12%	Britain
59	Colgate	4,602	4,572	1%	US
60	Philips	4,561	4,900	−7%	Netherlands
61	Nestle	4,430	N/A	N/A	Switzerland
62	Avon	4,399	4,369	1%	US
63	AOL	4,326	4,495	−4%	US
64	Chanel	4,272	4,265	0%	France
65	Kraft	4,079	4,032	1%	US
66	Danone	4,054	N/A	N/A	France
67	Yahoo!	3,855	4,378	−12%	US
68	adidas	3,690	3,650	1%	Germany
69	Rolex	3,686	3,701	0%	Switzerland
70	Time	3,682	3,724	−1%	US
71	Ericsson	3,589	7,069	−49%	Sweden
72	Tiffany & Co.	3,482	3,483	0%	US
73	Levi's	3,454	3,747	−8%	US
74	Motorola	3,416	3,761	−9%	US

Table 3.1 (continued)

2002 Ranking	Brand	2002 Brand Value ($MM)	2001 Brand Value ($MM)	% change, 2001–2002	Country of Owner- ship
75	Duracell	3,409	4,140	−18%	US
76	BP	3,390	3,247	4%	Britain
77	Hertz	3,362	3,617	−7%	US
78	Bacardi	3,341	3,204	4%	Bermuda
79	Caterpillar	3,218	N/A	N/A	US
80	Amazon.com	3,175	3,130	1%	US
81	Panasonic	3,141	3,490	−10%	Japan
82	Boeing	2,973	4,060	−27%	US
83	Shell	2,810	2,844	−1%	Britain/ Netherlands
84	Smirnoff	2,723	2,594	5%	US
85	Johnson & Johnson	2,509	N/A	N/A	US
86	Prada	2,489	N/A	N/A	Italy
87	Moet & Chandon	2,445	2,470	−1%	France
88	Heineken	2,396	2,266	6%	Germany
89	Mobil	2,358	2,415	−2%	US
90	Burger King	2,163	2,426	−11%	US
91	Nivea	2,059	1,782	16%	Britain
92	Wall Street Journal	1,961	2,184	−10%	US
93	Starbucks	1,961	1,757	12%	US
94	Barbie	1,937	2,037	−5%	US
95	Polo Ralph Lauren	1,928	1,910	1%	US
96	FedEx	1,919	1,885	2%	US
97	Johnnie Walker	1,654	1,649	0%	Britain
98	Jack Daniels	1,580	1,583	0%	US
99	3M	1,579	N/A	N/A	US
100	Armani	1,509	1,490	1%	Italy

To add to this, consumers, it seems, are becoming resistant to certain forms of traditional communication and as a result increasingly more difficult to reach as the media landscape explodes into a myriad of different distribution channels, new and old. All you need to do to confirm this phenomenon is to walk into any bookstore, or turn on your satellite or cable decoder, or drive down the highway from your home into the city. Consumers are being spoken to by advertisers at an ever-increasing rate and they are starting to get, at best, disillusioned . . . or, at worst, 'turned off'.

As such, it is becoming more and more difficult to stand out these days and the role of the brand is becoming more and more important as a store of consumer trust.

Brands also continue to be great stores of shareholder value. The amazing thing is that the accountants of the world, long immune to this realization, are at last starting to recognize that brands do carry a value and, as a result, we are starting to see the value of brands being disclosed on company balance sheets more formally; on a wide ranging basis this will only continue into the not too distant future.

The reality is that an increasingly large percentage of many global companies' market capitalization is comprised of the value of its brands, which have in effect become those companies' most valuable assets despite their intangible nature. Interestingly enough, it is not just the old established brands that hog the limelight. A number of relatively young brands also enjoy high brand values with the likes of Nike, Intel, Microsoft, Apple, Ikea and Nokia featuring prominently on brand valuation tables.

We also live in a world where consumers are becoming more and more concerned about the world and about their personal terms of reference in daily living and in the way that companies interact with that world and with them as people. The most exciting potential that brands present however must be their ability to act as a lighthouse to consumers in a cluttered world. They become symbols of what a company stands for and its value system. Brands that are responsive to this trend and connect with their consumers' passions and interests in a responsible and caring way are the ones that will thrive and succeed in the future.

So, with brands playing an increasingly important role marketers should be looking for new and innovative ways to build their brands. Passion branding provides marketers with one such powerful brand building tool with the ability to positively impact upon brand equity in a number of ways.

Leading Thought
Sean O'Neill, *Brand and Market Communication Director, Diageo*

I believe that brands will always be important to the consumer.

The good brands will grow in importance simply because as you get to understand and know the consumer better, you can deliver things that are truly of value to them. Conversely, the consumer has a finite amount of space in their lives and their minds to think about brands. Ultimately, they will increasingly use and buy the brands that are most relevant to them in their lives and which deliver against what they think is important and relevant.

So in important areas of life, I don't believe that consumers are after general commodity. I think they will, in those important areas such as sociability and leisure, opt for brands that clearly deliver against what's relevant and important to them.

Passion branding at the heart of brand building

So what is it that makes passion branding such a powerful ally of the brand builder in the passion economy?

Connecting with the whole person

Passion branding has the unique ability to empower a brand to connect with the whole person, not just the part of the person that consumes the brand. The potential for a brand, through passion branding, to establish an emotional bond with its consumers must surely rate as one of the most exciting opportunities faced by marketers in the last fifty years.

Leading Thought
Chris Weil, *Chairman and Chief Executive, Momentum Worldwide*

As a marketer why wouldn't you use sponsorship? What better medium is there? With sponsorship, you already have a loyal, passionate consumer following of whatever that sponsorship is, whether it's music or football or sailing – you already have a connection with the consumer. So if the fan that has the passion for something is the same person that is your consumer, why would you not borrow some of that equity and use that as the essence of an idea around which to build your communication?

3D Permission Marketing
– anticipated, personal and relevant

We all know how many marketing messages we are exposed to on a daily basis. From the moment you wake up to the to the time you close your eyes and fall asleep at night, marketers have found their way into just about every little thing we do whether it be the pages of a magazine, a billboard, radio, television, the internet, the bus and even the urinals in public places. You name it and the chances are that someone has thought of it as a space that an advertiser can try and interrupt whatever it is that you might be doing at the time.

Consumers have however come up with their own way of dealing with the thousands of interruptions that they receive each day. They simply ignore the messages, cut them out without even consciously knowing so. This is bad news for marketers trying to sell their products and services through traditional advertising methods. It is good news though to marketers who have cottoned on to the power of permission marketing, those marketers who show some respect for their consumers and only talk to them when invited to do so.

Internet marketing pioneer Seth Godin[4] talks about 'turning strangers into friends and friends into customers'. He claims that his approach works

---

[4]   Seth Godin, *Permission Marketing: Turning strangers into friends and friends into customers* (New York; Simon & Schuster: 1999).

because it 'speaks to people in an environment in which communication is anticipated, personal and relevant', and he makes a compelling argument backed up by solid examples of companies that are effectively using his approach. Much of Godin's proposition is based on the use of technology such as emails and the internet as a permission marketing platform. What I would like to do is to apply Godin's thinking to the world of passion branding and add to it by suggesting that passion branding is a form of permission marketing, but in 3D.

The three permission factors that Godin highlights, applied to passion branding, make for a compelling case:

Anticipated

Fans know that the sponsors of their passion are making a difference by making a contribution that makes it possible for them to enjoy their passion to the full. Fans also know, and accept, that sponsors are part and parcel of the environment in which they consume their passions and as such they anticipate them being there, in fact welcome them where the fan experience has been enhanced.

Relevant

The fact that a fan has elected to either participate in or watch an activity provides a high degree of relevance to that fan. If they weren't interested in the first place then they wouldn't be concerned with it. So, immediately, you are past the gate and through the door and on the way to their hearts.

Personal

Fans take a personal interest in the activities that they choose to follow; all that changes is the degree. The result of the game, the performance of their favourite athlete and so on, all have an impact. In many cases, it does not get more personal. As a sponsor, you are therefore talking to fans in a very personal environment.

The long and the short of all of this is that fans are more receptive to messages from brands in a passion branding environment than they are, for instance, to traditional above-the-line advertising where the advertisements are seen as an intrusion, adding little value to the viewer's experience.

The beauty of passion branding is that the consumer provides the marketer with permission to interact with them not only in bits and bytes but also in real life. As a permission marketing platform therefore, passion branding provides a marketer with access to a myriad number of consumer touch points that can be accessed and turned on for the benefit of the marketer's brand and business.

But a word of caution. As easily as consumers can regard traditional advertising as an intrusion in their lives, so too can they reject the overtures of sponsors who exploit the passion branding environment for their own selfish ends without adding any value to the fan experience. There is a fine balance between doing it right and over doing it. Cross the line and you will find your sponsorship spend as ineffective as your traditional advertising. The moment you lose a fan's permission is the moment that the value of passion branding disappears. Treat the fan's permission as the most valuable component of a passion branding campaign for without it, the greatest fit and strategy will not be worth the paper it is written on.

Leading Thought
Lawrence Flanagan, *Executive Vice President and Chief Marketing Officer for Global Marketing, MasterCard International*

The important thing is to identify where sponsorship falls in the chain of your marketing mix and marketing plan. I look at sponsorship as a marketing channel through which one can talk to specific consumer groups against whatever specific affinity or passion they might have, be that baseball or soccer for example. Understanding your consumers' affinities, interests and passions is therefore central to being able to open up this channel and being able to talk to your consumers in a language that they are attuned to.

MasterCard is involved with World Cup Soccer for example for two reasons; a combination of firstly its 'affinity' – despite the diversity of peoples around the world the event is something that millions of consumers can relate to, connect to and are passionate about; and secondly its 'scope' – it is one of the few remaining platforms that allows one to adopt a basic traditional mass-market approach. If you pair these two factors up with our brand strategy, World Cup Soccer becomes a very effective strategic channel for us to talk to our consumers. World Cup Soccer also reinforces our brand positioning – 'the best way to pay for everything that matters' – which we execute through our 'Priceless' campaign.

So our whole message to consumers is, 'it's not about what you buy, it's more important why you're buying it and what's important in your life'. World Cup is a passion, it's a huge passion, a priceless experience for many consumers – their country winning or simply being able to go to the World Cup are things that go beyond what money can buy; it's a vision or a dream which ties right in to our brand positioning that 'there are some things money can't buy. For everything else there's MasterCard'.

The whole passion around World Cup therefore provides us with a perfect platform for us to communicate our message.

Leading marketing writer Adam Morgan adds a further dimension to the potential that sponsorship provides to marketers, in particular for challenger brands, those brands that need their own set of marketing rules if they are to have any hope of staying afloat and competing effectively against the leader in their category.[5]

Leading Thought
Adam Morgan, *Eating the Big Fish*

One of the things that I am most interested in with regard to challenger brands, is the whole issue of intensity. My view is that the only clarity for a challenger brand is strong preference. If you have weak preference or parity preference, all the other things that a market leader has on their side like the general ubiquity, the general social acceptability, R & D, distribution, all those things are going to kick in. So what you need to do as a challenger brand is to create intense preference, and part of that is going to be about the kind of message that you communicate.

---

[5] Adam Morgan, *Eating the Big Fish: How Challenger Brands can compete against brand leaders* (London: John Wiley & Sons: 1999).

The whole idea of challenger brands having a lighthouse identity is that they have a very clear sense about where they stand in the world and they have a very clear point of view about the world and what's important and what is not important, and they project that very intensely in everything they do.

The interesting question then is, as a challenger brand, how do you find media that is a natural complement to that desire to communicate intensely and build intense relationships? The interesting thing about sponsorship is, where else do you find people who are responding in their environment or feeling at their most intense about a particular area or a particular subject which is important to them? It's actually very rare that people have an intense relationship with their media environment. The potential that sponsorship offers therefore of being in a place where people are having a very strong and intense emotional connection with what's going on in front of them and how one weaves one into that experience through passion branding, has some interesting implications.

For challenger brands, sponsorship is therefore an under-appreciated tool particularly if you can imaginatively interweave yourself into that experience rather than simply strap yourself onto the side of it in some kind of way; I think that becomes really interesting.

Emotions – real, not borrowed

One of my greatest criticisms of traditional above-the-line communication is that more often than not, the emotions drawn on by the creatives in production are at best borrowed and at worst manufactured. As such the advertising is grounded on image rather than substance, which any savvy consumer will see right through.

Conversely, passion branding provides the platform for themed communications using emotions that are real, not borrowed. This immediately gives the communication credibility in the eyes of the consumer particularly given the added value that the brand or company will be providing in the process.

One company that has done a particularly good job while using this approach is SAB Miller, the world's second largest brewer with 111 breweries in 24 countries. Castle Lager is the company's leading beer in the South African market and has three core pillars to its brand identity, one of which centres around national pride through its positioning as the 'great South African beer', truly representative of the nation's aspirations. As an extension of this positioning, Castle Lager is the major sponsor of the national soccer, rugby and cricket teams, and uses this association with the country's three most popular sports as a platform around which its above the line communication is themed. In so doing, Castle draws on the national pride of the South African population and the passionate and patriotic emotions that go hand in hand with this pride are transferred to the Castle Lager brand.

By placing its sponsorship at the centre of Castle Lager's brand building efforts, SAB Miller is able to leverage its investment across a range of integrated communications activities and generate a significantly greater return on its communication investments than would be the case if it had approached each element of its communication as a stand-alone exercise.

MasterCard is another brand that believes in this approach as is evidenced through the following great example of how a sponsorship can be used as a central platform off which a myriad of communication activities can be launched. Through baseball, MasterCard has aligned itself with a sponsorship platform that is highly relevant to its American customers and uses the sponsorship environment to talk to its consumers using the MasterCard brand language in a way that is consistent with MasterCard's overall brand strategy.

CASE STUDY

MasterCard Major League Baseball Memorable Moments

Baseball is fondly regarded as 'America's favourite pastime' and therefore presents a powerful platform for MasterCard to use to connect with US consumers in particular and with baseball fans worldwide. By linking its brand to a sport that consumers have a passion for, MasterCard is able to tap into that passion and claim some transfer to its brand. But the true success of the association lies in MasterCard's leverage of the sponsorship. Rather than merely using the designation, 'Proud Sponsor of Major League Baseball', MasterCard fully embraces the sponsorship platform by integrating it into the overall communications mix and creating various leverage extensions off it.

Each year, as part of MasterCard's baseball sponsorship, the company initiates a major promotional programme in conjunction with Major League Baseball which aims to provide an opportunity for MasterCard cardholders to gain exclusive access to something that is 'priceless' and that they would not be able to get without MasterCard, simply by using their card.

In 2002 MasterCard embarked on the Memorable Moments promotion. This was a season-long promotion whereby fans around the world could relive their favourite memories of the game and vote for their top five greatest moments in baseball history via on-line and off-line balloting. In addition, consumers using their MasterCard card any time from July 9th, when the promotion was launched, to September 20th, were automatically entered to win a once-in-a-lifetime opportunity to participate in the Memorable Moments celebration at the 2002 World Series.

The promotion was launched on July 9th through a spectacular on-field ceremony prior to the All Star Game and was televised live on FOX TV. A panel of experts, made up of baseball executives, members of the media, baseball historians and even US President George W. Bush, had selected the top 30 moments in baseball history and these were announced to the nation at the ceremony. Many of the living legends who participated in these memorable moments also made an appearance and received rousing ovations for their contributions to America's favourite pastime.

Fan ballots were distributed via all 30 Major League Baseball ballparks, various magazines including *Sports Illustrated*, *Rolling Stone* and *American Way* (American Airlines in-flight magazine), Best Western Hotels, BJ's Wholesale Clubs, The Sports Authority and via the internet.

MasterCard's overall objective for the promotion was to drive awareness and brand preference to ultimately increase MasterCard usage. In order to achieve this MasterCard identified the following, more specific objectives:

• Drive national consumer awareness of MasterCard and its sponsorship of Memorable Moments through an integrated marketing plan.

- Leverage the emotion associated with Major League Baseball to connect with MasterCard cardholders.
- Extend relationship with MasterCard key merchants and member partners.
- Increase positive perception and relevance of the MasterCard brand through 'Priceless' advertising.

The programme was fully integrated across a number of channels from media and public relations to member banks and merchants. Major baseball events were utilized as platforms to launch and promote the programme and club support, through the distribution of ballots and PA announcements, helped to generate awareness of, and interest in, the promotion across the USA.

Throughout the promotion 176 MasterCard member financial institutions showed their support with customized statement inserts, in-branch merchandising kits, premiums and co-branded websites as well as balloting and sweepstakes point-of-sale materials and licensed merchandise sales.

In conjunction with the promotion, MasterCard ran a baseball themed 'Priceless' commercial featuring great moments in the history of American baseball such as Lou Garrett's farewell message and Henry Aaron hitting the 750th home run. The commercial culminated in the MasterCard pay-off line – 'Our past time – Priceless'. It was a highly emotional commercial that recognized the role that baseball plays in American society and was a powerful motivator for people to vote for their most memorable baseball moment.

Major League Baseball also played a key role in the overall integrated marketing effort and supported the programme via television, print, radio and in-stadium advertising and through significant presence on MLB.com, including the on-line voting and photos and video clips of the Memorable Moments. In addition, MLB also chronicled the 30 Memorable Moments in a five-part series of one-hour specials which were aired exclusively on ESPN.

All votes were tallied and the top 10 Memorable Moments were individually announced on October 7th at a dramatic on-field ceremony prior to game four of the World Series. The occasion was televised live on FOX TV and the winning Memorable Moment, that of Cal Ripken Junior's historic 2,131st consecutive game played was celebrated by fans at the stadium and around the world.

Results

MasterCard's Memorable Moments promotion was recognized by top league officials as the 'most significant marketing campaign ever initiated by Major League Baseball and one of its business partners' and its immense success can be seen on a number of levels.

Advertising

The Memorable Moments TV commercial was MasterCard's best performing baseball-themed commercial spot to date and registered an Awareness Index of 10 amongst baseball enthusiasts and 8 among the general sample.

Previous advertising campaigns such as 'The Trip' and 'All Century Team' executions scored 4 amongst the general sample and 6 among baseball enthusiasts.

Media

The promotion resulted in the following added value through media buys: 32 per cent increase in value from television cost and a 93 per cent increase in value from print cost. 92 per cent of the media coverage included MasterCard key messages and 27 per cent of the coverage was in 'A-list' media. The value of the media support behind the campaign amounted to $30.6 million.

National usage sweepstakes

More than 175 member banks and 350,000 merchant locations participated in the promotion and sweepstakes with fully integrated support from MLB and MasterCard.

Member bank promotions

Member participation was the deepest acceptance of a MasterCard promotion in all three member groups to date. More than 49 million promotional inserts and mailers were distributed to cardholders and potential prospects during the promotional period.

Merchant promotions

Nine nationally recognized category leaders from eight unique merchant channels participated in the programme. Over 3 million ballots were distributed via the merchant partners. Among the nine merchant participants MasterCard GDV increased by 64.5 per cent and average transactions increased by 64.1 per cent during the promotional period against a year ago.

Fan balloting

Over 21 million ballots were distributed during the promotion, one of the largest post-All Star game Major League Baseball balloting programmes ever. More than 1.5 million votes were tallied online. All 30 MLB clubs conducted Memorable Moments balloting in their ballparks.

Club marketing

All MasterCard clubs supported the programme via ballot distribution and collection, video board promotion and live PA announcements. A selection of baseball personalities contributed to local promotions including Carlton Fisk (Boston Red Sox), Ozzie Smith (St. Louis Cardinals) and Hank Aaron (Atlanta Braves).

Public relations

Among the personalities retained to drive increased awareness for MasterCard and emphasize the usage component were Barry Bonds, Ozzie Smith, Carlton Fisk, Willie Mays, Ralph Branca, Bobby Thompson, Tim McCarver, Reggie Jackson, Luis Gonzalez and Cal Ripken Jr. Combined public relations activities generated 260 print stories, 225 broadcast stories and 217,106,573 media impressions.

Internet

MasterCard's online activities resulted in 105 million internet impressions. The promotion resulted in 485 registrations for mastercard.com.

Hispanic outreach

For the first time, all of the components of a MasterCard national programme were translated into Spanish, including TV, print and online media components.

International

Participation from Latin America and Asia/Pacific resulted in the largest number of worldwide impressions ever garnered by a MasterCard promotion.

KEY INSIGHT

The success of MasterCard's sponsorship is a combination of a clear brand positioning, together with a thorough understanding of its consumers' passions and

then bringing the sponsorship relationship to bear upon these factors through a
totally integrated sponsorship leverage programme.

Leading Thought
Patrick Magyar, *Chief Executive, FIFA Marketing AG*

What we have noted is that the FIFA World Cup generates a different kind of passion than just football. For example, there are many people who watch the FIFA World Cup, particularly women, who never watch league matches etc. Why? Because the FIFA World Cup has elevated itself from being a sports event to being a passionate, cultural, social relevant event.

This has a lot to do with the equity of the event itself. I think that having a team like Brazil play against Germany in the final, generates passion, generates emotion all over the world even if your own team is not playing. This is the interesting thing – the strength of the FIFA World Cup is that you become part of it – you favour one against the other one. You're not connected at all with these countries.

People identify and want to be part of the event and we see that in the public viewing that we have. There's never in sport been an event where as many people watch the event together in public areas or at work or together with friends, than this time. We had in Korea for example, for the semi final, more than 7 million people on the road watching in public viewing areas which is a huge amount compared to the 25.4 million that watched it on TV at home. It is this kind of togetherness that creates around the FIFA World Cup, the largest 'we' group in the world. There's no social movement or phenomenon that is as big as the FIFA World Cup in the sense of human beings it touches emotionally and makes them feel part of one big family.

The results that we have received from our consumer research shows a wish or a readiness amongst fans to change to our partners brands of over 16 per cent. In my knowledge, any other sponsorship never comes close to half of that. So, the huge advantage with the FIFA World Cup is that when you touch people with FIFA World Cup you immediately capture their hearts. People don't buy FIFA World Cup merchandise because they just like the emblem or something like that – it's because they identify with this kind of event and to its sponsors because it is real and has a special place in their lives.

Contributing towards brand equity

If a brand is something that exists in the mind of your consumers, let us take a look at the numerous ways in which passion branding contributes towards developing the consumer's perception of your brand.

Brand loyalty

Perhaps the most powerful attribute of passion branding is its ability to develop consumer brand loyalty in such a way that positively influences purchasing behaviour. Simply put, passion branding has the power to influence purchasing behaviour.

If the key to brand profits is in the customers mind[6] then what passion branding does is to place the sponsoring brand at the centre of the consumer's passion and in the process earns the right to a share of mind.

People are all about likes and dislikes, needs and aspirations, dreams and hopes, passions and interests. When a brand identifies with these same factors, that person is more likely to treat that brand as one of the family.

Passion branding therefore provides fertile ground for marketers as a result of its ability to place a brand right alongside its consumers in an environment where they are passionate about what it is that they are doing and therefore receptive to messages from friendly sponsors. Further, the fact that consumers often benefit directly from the sponsor's support makes it easier for them to support the sponsor in return with their loyalty. Correctly positioned, sponsors have the potential to become part of the 'team'.

Some recent research out of the US makes for interesting reading. 'NASCAR[7] fans provide one of the highest levels of brand loyalty and sponsorship support of any one of the hundred or so sports and special events that we've tested,' says Jed Pearsall, Performance Research.[8]

---

[6]   Jan Hofmeyer & Butch Rice, *Commitment Led Marketing* (West Sussex; John Wiley & Sons Ltd; 2000).

[7]   National Association for Stock Car Auto Racing – the most popular type of motorsport in the US.

[8]   *Loyal NASCAR Fans Please Stand Up*. Case study available on the Performance Research website (http://www.performanceresearch.com).

Over 1,000 nationwide random NASCAR fans were interviewed by Performance Research and 57 per cent indicated that they had higher trust in products offered by NASCAR sponsors than non-NASCAR sponsors. 71 per cent of NASCAR fans reported that they almost always or frequently choose a product involved in NASCAR over one that is not, simply because of the sponsorship.

Another motor sport-related passion branding campaign that brings to life the power of sponsorship as a loyalty builder is that of Shell's sponsorship of Ferrari. It is a great example of how an association with a passion brand can be leveraged to maximum effect on a global basis.

CASE STUDY

Shell's sponsorship of Ferrari Formula One: tapping into fan passion on a global scale

Oil and Petroleum brands, by their very nature, do not enjoy a high degree of emotional affinity with customers. The challenge for such brands is therefore to partner with passion brands and leverage the association so that some of the emotional attachment associated with the passion brand rubs off onto the blander fuel brand. This is the central motivation behind Shell's sponsorship of Ferrari. Shell's Vice President of Global Brands, Raoul Pinnell explains – 'It's an association with a passion brand. If we as a brand with lower levels of emotional affinity can get some of that emotional attachment to us then that will add to our brand.'

Shell has a long and proud association with Formula One, having been involved with the sport since the World Championship was launched in 1950. The current contract with Ferrari is due to run until 2005 and entails a significant annual investment.

Shell's alignment with the emotionally powerful Ferrari team and its dominant driver, Michael Schumacher, represents the most appropriate and credible global sponsorship vehicle for Shell. The Formula One circuit is made up of 17 races around the world over an eight-month period and is watched by a global audience of more than 350 million people in 190 countries. The Shell brand is equally far reaching with a presence in 135 countries, 48,000 retail sites and 20 million customers daily. Formula One is therefore a highly effective global billboard for Shell and has an important role to play in driving Shell's global brand consistency.

Formula One is also an excellent platform for Shell to test its powerful research and development capabilities, demonstrate its product attributes, convey a brand leadership position and engender customer loyalty in this parity market where customer choice is driven more by the location of the forecourt than by any emotional connection with the brand.

Shell's strategic objectives in sponsoring Ferrari are to:

- Shift consumer brand preference and loyalty from competitors to Shell, by using the Ferrari association, to make Shell the leading aspirational brand in automotive fuels and lubricants.
- Position Shell as the market leader in product technology, quality and value by communicating Shell's use of Formula One and Ferrari as a laboratory for new product development and a proving ground for current products.
- Create a high level of awareness and strong image for Shell premium product brands such as Shell Helix Ultra motor oil, especially in launch markets.
- Encourage product sampling, purchase and loyalty among consumers by adding Formula One-related incentives to Shell loyalty programmes, retail promotions and media promotions where appropriate.
- Enhance relations with, and support from, key business audiences, including the oil trade, motor industry, media, business community, government sector and employees.

Shell is well aware that buying the rights is only the starting point and that the real value is derived from effective sponsorship exploitation. To this end, Shell maximizes both the technical aspects of its association with Ferrari and the brand exposure elements. In terms of the technical elements, Shell supplies fuels and lubricants to the team and contributes towards technical research and development. The inherent value of this is that it is a credible demonstration to the customer of Shell's performance capabilities and it drives a leadership position in a powerful way.

From a marketing perspective, Shell's alignment with Ferrari is integrated with the global brand strategy and communication campaigns. Shell uses a combination of on-car and trackside branding to take advantage of the television exposure to Formula One's 350 million television audience. Shell forecourts highlight the relationship through logo visibility or mentions on its products, on pump and on its tankers. Shell also uses media PR, the internet, hospitality, pit tours and access to the team and drivers for its customers, suppliers and staff, merchandise and various Formula One-themed promotions to exploit its association with Ferrari; all this ensures that the brand-vehicle relationship remains relevant and that the benefits of the association are maximized.

Key to the success of Shell's sponsorship is the consistent application of the sponsorship across all its markets globally. This is ensured through a management implementation plan and guidelines which are communicated to all operating units and set out the dos and don'ts with respect to leveraging the Shell Ferrari relationship.

In evaluating the success of the sponsorship, Shell makes use of a number of data sources and methodologies, predominantly the Shell Global Brand Tracker (GBT) and the Motorists Lubricants Tracker (MLT). These two tracking tools are essentially similar in nature in that they track annual usage and attitudes of private motorists, but the key differences are that the MLT looks at both retail and non-retail channels of trade, it looks at passenger car motor oils instead of retail fuels and asks only two simple questions as opposed to the more detailed 11-point allocation approach used in the Global Brand Tracker. Shell is particularly mindful of ensuring that the information revealed through these sources is linked to specific actionability and does not serve merely as a reference work.

Broadly speaking, the format used by Shell evaluates the sponsorship's impact on brand awareness and attitude and on claimed purchase behaviour, whether it be trial or repeat purchase; and a more detailed examination of specific sponsorship exploitation activities is also carried out, all of which culminates in a cost-benefit analysis and an assessment of the key learnings. The Shell global network is encouraged to share best practice to enhance sponsorship exploitation programmes in the various regions.

Table 3.2 Awareness of Shell's sponsorship of Ferrari. Reprinted with permission from Shell

	1997	1998	1999	2000	2001	2000/1 vs. 1998/9 % change
Europe	18%	19%	21%	21%	25%	+15%
South	16%	22%	22%	27%	30%	+30%
East	12%	12%	16%	15%	19%	+20%
Global	15%	17%	18%	19%	22%	+20%

The success of Shell's partnership is evident on a number of levels:

- The Global Brand Tracker shows that global awareness of the sponsorship has increased by 20 per cent since 1997.
- Since Shell's latest decision to renew its relationship with Ferrari, in the majority of operating units, which account for 60 per cent of fuel volume, the levels of awareness have increased by an average of 35 per cent (2000–1 vs. 1998–9) and the impact on overall preference share was 0.15 percentage points.
- Reassuringly, the MLT shows very similar levels of awareness of Shell's sponsorship of Ferrari (globally 24 per cent compared with the GBT's 22 per cent awareness levels).
- The differences in share of preference between those who are unaware of the sponsorship and those who are aware, are very consistent across both the GBT and the MLT despite the different methodologies used. Both MLT questions show preference levels amongst those aware to be 18 per cent higher than among those who are not, whereas in the GBT the percentage difference is 17 per cent.
- The MLT data shows strong linkages, in behaviour and attitudes towards Shell's sponsorship. The differences in attitude between those aware of the sponsorship and those unaware are particularly noticeable when dealing with extreme driving conditions and expert associations.

Table 3.3 Awareness of Shell's Sponsorship of Ferrari (changes since decision to re-sign, years 2000/1 compared with 1998/9). Reprinted with permission from Shell

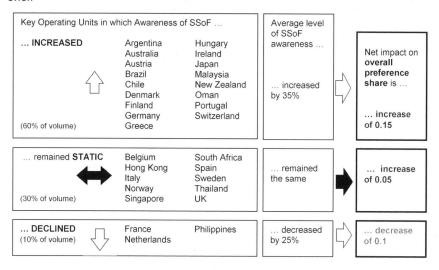

Table 3.4 Linkage of Awareness of Shell's Sponsorship of Ferrari with Preference. Reprinted with permission from Shell

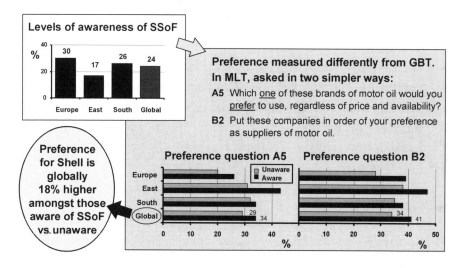

Table 3.5 Linkage of Shell's sponsorship of Ferrari with behaviour and perceptions. Reprinted with permission from Shell

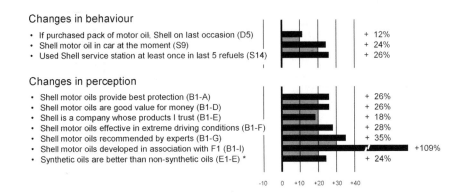

Differences between those aware of SSoF vs. unaware

Changes in behaviour
- If purchased pack of motor oil, Shell on last occasion (D5)   + 12%
- Shell motor oil in car at the moment (S9)   + 24%
- Used Shell service station at least once in last 5 refuels (S14)   + 26%

Changes in perception
- Shell motor oils provide best protection (B1-A)   + 26%
- Shell motor oils are good value for money (B1-D)   + 26%
- Shell is a company whose products I trust (B1-E)   + 18%
- Shell motor oils effective in extreme driving conditions (B1-F)   + 28%
- Shell motor oils recommended by experts (B1-G)   + 35%
- Shell motor oils developed in association with F1 (B1-I)   +109%
- Synthetic oils are better than non-synthetic oils (E1-E) *   + 24%

-10   0   +10   +20   +30   +40

The strength of Shell's alignment with Ferrari in terms of creating greater emotional affinity towards the Shell brand is also evident in comments from Shell customers and Formula One fans around the globe. This is what some of them have said of the relationship:

- 'Both are world leaders – no. 1 in their field' – Canada.
- 'There are no negatives. Ferrari and Shell both go together and there is combined potential for improvement' – Thailand.
- 'I use Shell so that my taxi can go like a Ferrari' – Taxi driver, South Africa.
- 'Shell gives Ferrari strength' – Saudi Arabia.
- 'Shell needs Ferrari a lot more than Ferrari needs Shell' – USA.
- 'The F1 connection demands good lubrication, everything working well in the engine, no crap in the fuel. Ferrari is top quality and top quality demands top quality' – Thailand.

KEY INSIGHT

In order to fully capitalize on the emotional affinity a fan has for a passion brand there should be a plausible link between the sponsor and the passion brand to which it is aligned. The more credible the link, the greater the potential to fully exploit the relationship and gain maximum benefit from it. In the case of a global passion brand, ensure that it is consistently exploited across all regions so that consumers everywhere have the same clear understanding of what you are trying to communicate through the association.

Some additional insight into the link between fan loyalty and passion branding is offered by international research company SRI and their work for a mobile (cell) phone handset brand around its sponsorship of soccer in the UK. What is evident from SRI's findings is that the best examples of passion branding are those where the alignment or fit between the sponsoring brand and the fans is most relevant and personal. Given the sponsor's objectives in this case, it was not just about sponsoring soccer but rather about sponsoring soccer at the right level, at club level, as opposed to at national team level.

What is very evident however is that brand loyalty can only be garnered through passion branding activities where the passion brander's motivations are genuine, adds value to the fans' interaction with their passion and is authentic. This is a theme that many of the thought leaders that I spoke to reinforced and one that Harlan Stone further explains.

Leading Thought
Harlan Stone, *Principal, VelocitySports & Entertainment*

Fans need to be both passionate about the activity and feel authenticity behind any sponsorship to be truly motivated from a loyalty prospective. Fans will not necessarily be loyal to a big sponsor of an event if that sponsor a) doesn't speak to them b) isn't involved authentically in the sport (i.e. does their sponsorship make sense and does their particular activation plan really work?). As an example, in the United States it's very easy to see the authenticity and passion that Gatorade has in its sponsorships – there's a natural editorial linkage between athletes working very hard sweating and needing to replenish with the right isotonic – and this commitment and authenticity has come through all of Gatorade's branding efforts including their advertising. What is less clear is when a company like CONAGRA – a food distributor – puts its name on the Skins game, a made-for-TV golf tournament. Consumers are too smart to become passionate about a brand that doesn't have editorial authenticity and has no reach to them.

Brand awareness and attention

There is definitely a benefit in being ubiquitous, just ask Coca-Cola, and passion branding provides a wonderful cost-effective means of putting a brand up in lights and in front of consumers. As brand guru David Aaker says, 'People like the familiar and are prepared to ascribe all sorts of good attitudes to items that are familiar to them'.

Enhanced awareness has long been one of the key objectives sought by sponsors and is still in many cases the only benefit sought.

Passion branding provides a cost-effective way of driving awareness for a brand at a fraction of the budget that would be required to achieve the same results using traditional advertising methods. Western Union's broadcast sponsorship of the *World of Soccer* is a good example and is covered in Chapter 5 in some detail.

Passion branding is particularly effective in driving awareness for a brand at launch or re-launch as Vodafone demonstrated with their sponsorships of Ferrari and Formula One and Manchester United FC, two hugely popular passion brands.

Brand attributes and benefits

As Passion branding is based on real activities, it provides the perfect setting to demonstrate brand attributes and benefits directly to consumers.

Consumers can be afforded the opportunity to 'test drive' a brand first-hand in a passion branding setting and therefore arrive at their own conclusions as to its usefulness. By placing the brand at the heart of the sponsored activity, as for example IBM has successfully done for years around the Olympic Games as the official technology partner of the Games, the fans' consumption of their passion can be enhanced with positive spillover benefits for the sponsoring brand.

IBM's Surf Shack, for example, provided athletes at the Nagano Winter Olympics with the opportunity to test first hand IBM's technology while keeping in touch with friends, family and fans through email and the internet. This experience will far outweigh and outlive any demonstration that IBM might have undertaken of their technology through, for example, some kind of traditional above-the-line advertising campaign.

Consumers are therefore relieved of the onus of having to rely only on advertising claims in advance of purchasing a brand.

Passion branding also provides a wonderful platform from which a sponsoring brand can demonstrate its various features in an environment where consumers are more open to try out things and less suspicious of the sponsoring brand's intentions.

CASE STUDY

Flora London Marathon 2001

Since 1996, Flora's brand performances have varied, with the *Light* and *pro.activ* variants experiencing growth while the *Original* and *Buttery* have declined. As a whole, Flora holds a steady and dominant market share but, overall, the margarine/butter category has experienced a decline of roughly 2 per cent per annum.

In order to counteract the effect of a declining 'spreads' market and rebuild an emotional connection with consumers, Flora sponsors the popular annual London Marathon and uses this platform to credibly promote the link between the health benefits of the brand and the importance of exercise as part of a healthy, well-balanced lifestyle.

The event primarily targets women with children who think they should concentrate more on their health as well as adults, over 55 years, who are actively seeking to reduce their cholesterol level (Flora *pro.activ* consumers). Every year the London Marathon attracts almost 80,000 entries and accepts over 40,000 runners, of which there are at least 30,000 finishers.

Flora's sponsorship objectives are as follows:

- Education: increasing awareness of, and belief in, Flora's health benefits.
- Rebuild an emotional relationship between the brand and consumers, 'Make people love Flora'.

- Drive specific PR messages that create positive brand associations, e.g.,
  - *Flora helps maintain a healthy heart,*
  - *Flora is good for the whole family,*
  - *Flora is a brand that cares for people's health.*

The sponsorship becomes the central theme for all of Flora's marketing communications and is leveraged effectively in a number of ways. In 2001 Flora made use of two high profile British Olympians, Sir Steve Redgrave and Tanni Grey Thompson who were actively 'pushed' to the media from both a training and participation perspective prior to, and around, the event. In addition, media partners were secured which ensured effective reach of the sponsorship messaging. *The Times* published a Flora London Marathon supplement which contained good branding and some editorial control. The radio partner, Capital Radio, provided extensive coverage prior to and during the event including outside broadcasts and even had one of its DJs competing in the event. The BBC covered the event on television.

From a PR perspective various activities were undertaken which aimed to extend the reach and longevity of the sponsorship. A regional photographic tour was arranged, which saw a 'behind the scenes' photography exhibition visit 13 high profile fitness centres nationwide. FLM21.co.uk, a website created for race competitors, was publicized through national media and regional radio stations. In addition a fancy-dress competition for race participants was initiated with judging taking place during the event. Radio competitions were held during the week after the race which encouraged regular and sustained exercise.

Above-the-line activity consisted of a television, press, PR and outdoor campaign focusing on Flora *pro.activ* and the brand's endorsement by Sir Steve Redgrave.

From a retail perspective, Flora initiated a competition with three major supermarket chains around the UK. The supermarkets provided extensive point-of-sale material and 'at fixture' competitions which resulted in increased activity nationally, as well as specifically within stores on the race route.

Internally, staff also benefited from the sponsorship and a limited number were granted the right to participate in the event. A further benefit was the opportunity to purchase Adidas kit at discounted prices as well as access to the hospitality area on race day.

The Flora London Marathon has a positive effect on the Flora brand and the media coverage that the event generates provides a solid platform for conveying the desired Flora brand messages. Some of the key effects and outputs from the 2001 event are as follows:

- Live BBC coverage for 5.25 hours received average viewing figures of 4.4 million and Flora brand exposure during the broadcast rose from 118 minutes in 2000 to 194 minutes in 2001.
- A significant portion of the audience fell under the Flora *pro.activ* consumer target (27 per cent of the television audience were 65+).
- Press coverage spanned national newspapers (55 articles), regionals (222 articles) as well as consumer and trade press (31 and 10 articles respectively).
- Sir Steve Redgrave's participation in the event created almost 40 per cent of total press coverage.
- Those aware of Flora's association with the London Marathon gave higher awareness ratings for Flora's PR messages.
- The value share of the butter/margarine sector peaked at 19.3 per cent after the event within Safeway stores.

Such has been the success of Flora's sponsorship of the London Marathon, that Flora has extended its involvement in road running through title sponsorship of the Flora Light Challenge for Women, the largest annual female 5 km fun run in the UK which attracted a record 20,000 people in 2001. The sponsorship has also been extended to Sydney, Australia.

KEY INSIGHT

There is an obvious link between the brand messages that Flora wishes to convey and the benefits associated with exercise and road running which makes the London Marathon a powerful platform for the Flora brand. Furthermore, Flora exploits the sponsorship at various levels which adds to its overall reach and success.

Table 3.6 Awareness of Flora PR messaging amongst those aware of the sponsorship vs. those not aware of the sponsorship. Reprinted with permission from Unilever

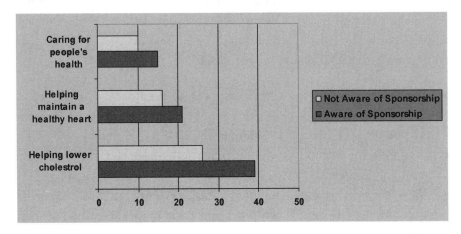

Brand associations and value exchange

While traditional advertising tends to borrow associations or create them fictitiously, sponsorship provides marketers with access to associations that are real and honest, ones that consumers have experienced first-hand and can therefore buy into.

For example, SAB Miller, the world's second largest beer company, have used sponsorships of the South African national sports teams to very effectively draw on the pride of the nation as depicted by South Africa's national rugby, soccer and cricket teams – and in the process have been able to position Castle Lager as a national icon in South Africa.

An association with a passion platform says a lot about a brand's relative position in the marketplace. An aspirant brand leader will derive substantial benefits from associating itself with an established market leading platform – not only from the association with the platform itself, but probably more importantly from the association with the other brand leaders who are co-sponsoring the event.

Hyundai, for example, as a result of its sponsorship of World Cup Soccer, benefits tremendously not only from its association with one of the greatest events in the world but also from its association with global mega brands like Coca-Cola and MasterCard who are also sponsors of the event.

CASE STUDY

Hyundai and the 2002 FIFA World Cup™

Using sponsorship to enhance a brand's global positioning

Founded in 1967, Hyundai Motor Company is relatively new when compared to the other major motor manufacturers. Nevertheless, in just over three decades, Hyundai has overcome the odds and earned global recognition for the advanced technology and quality of its automobiles to the extent that it is now the world's eighth largest automaker and is fast closing in on the global top five manufacturers.

Integral to the growth of the Hyundai brand has been the aggressive marketing strategy which it adopts. Hyundai uses the universally understood and emotively powerful language of sport, and in particular the world's largest sport, football, as the unifying theme at the core of its marketing activities.

Hyundai's association with football and the 2002 FIFA World Cup™ enabled the brand to primarily drive two key messages to consumers.

- Through an association with the world's largest sporting event which attracts an audience of over 35 billion people, Hyundai is able to create the impression that it is a mega brand with a larger global reach than is actually the case.

- As one of 15 multinational brands afforded the status of Official Partners of the 2002 FIFA World Cup™, Hyundai was positioned alongside world-class brand leaders such as Coca-Cola, McDonalds, MasterCard, Philips and Adidas which again helps to enhance Hyundai's global positioning as a competitive and respected player in its product category.

Hyundai took full advantage of its sponsorship of the 2002 FIFA World Cup™ in Korea by activating the sponsorship on a number of levels worldwide. The Hyundai brand experience was taken into the heart of the community in every key market, using leverage initiatives that actively engaged with consumers and aimed to build brand affinity, increase Hyundai's brand awareness and enhance the company's image.

The main leverage activities undertaken by Hyundai around the 2002 FIFA World Cup™ included three major programmes.

1. Hyundai Goodwill Ball Roadshow

The Hyundai Goodwill Ball Roadshow consisted of high-profile media events and interactive Hyundai experiences delivered in each of the 32 countries whose teams had qualified to participate in the 2002 FIFA World Cup™. The Roadshow kicked off with a media launch in Korea using 32 giant 4.5 metre branded balls which represented each country participating in the competition as well as one all-nations ball bearing the flags of all 32 competing countries. Fans were invited to sign good luck messages to their team on the ball and, during the tournament, the balls were positioned outside every stadium where the team competed which created a unique branding opportunity for Hyundai to distinguish itself from the other event sponsors.

More than 150 Goodwill Ball Roadshow events were held globally and it is estimated that over 1.6 million people were exposed to the Hyundai brand through these events. More than 130,000 good luck messages were signed on the balls and the events generated extensive national and international media coverage, with the launch alone attended by over 200 media representatives from around the world.

Consumers around the world also responded positively to the events, with 62 per cent saying that the roadshow had resulted in them having a more positive view of Hyundai; 72 per cent agreeing that they had been able to learn more about Hyundai's products through the events; 84 per cent saying that that they felt Hyundai had more interest in its consumers than prior to the event and 52 per cent saying that, having been exposed to Hyundai, they would consider buying the brand in the future.

Figure 3.1 Hyundai Goodwill Balls signed by fans. Reprinted with permission from Hyundai

Figure 3.2 Hyundai Goodwill Balls programme – the all-nations ball. Reprinted with permission from Hyundai

2. Hyundai Football World Championships

Hyundai initiated a grassroots amateur football programme to build credibility of the Hyundai brand worldwide. The Hyundai Football World Championships consisted of 5-a-side amateur football tournaments which were held regionally in 50 countries and then culminated in the World Final in Korea. In this way Hyundai was able to make the brand and its sponsorship of the 2002 FIFA World Cup™ accessible and relevant in both qualified and unqualified markets.

In total 5,000 teams and 40,000 players took part in these events. Media coverage was extensive with the World Final being screened live on 'SBS Korea' and with coverage on 'Western Union Football Show' which is broadcast worldwide to 120 countries. Consumer response was also positive with 66 per cent of participants saying that they had a more positive perception of Hyundai and 54 per cent saying that they would consider buying a Hyundai in future as a result of their exposure and involvement in the event.

3. Hyundai Ambassador Programme

Hyundai appointed Dutch footballing legend, Johan Cruyff, to act as an ambassador and to promote its association with the 2002 FIFA World Cup™ thereby building an affinity between the Hyundai brand and the target audience. Johan Cruyff is a revered global icon and his leadership and world-class qualities were a strong brand fit with the aspirations of the Hyundai Motor Corporation to become a leading global car manufacturer and its credibility.

Johan Cruyff was used by Hyundai at a number of functions in the build-up to and during the 2002 FIFA World Cup™. In all cases his presence created additional hype and newsworthiness and elevated the Hyundai brand. Some of these functions included the following:

- The international launch of the new Hyundai Coupé at the Frankfurt Motor Show.
- Joined Chairman of Hyundai Motor Company for the groundbreaking of the new European Headquarters to international media.
- Represented the Hyundai Motor Company as a guest of FIFA at the final draw for the 2002 FIFA World Cup™.
- Conducted over 100 media interviews and made over 5 international appearances, which resulted in coverage on CNN, Eurosport, Sky Sports, SBS Korea and China TV.
- Was used in distributor advertising and promotions in Asia, Europe and South America.

KEY INSIGHT

Although a relatively new brand in the motor vehicle manufacturer's category, Hyundai used the 2002 FIFA World Cup™ very effectively to enhance its brand profile and increase its global stature. Partnered alongside established world leading brands, such as Coca-Cola and Philips to name but two, and aligning with the world's biggest sporting event, provided the perfect platform for Hyundai to elevate itself in the eyes of consumers around the world and, thanks to a well-executed leverage programme which was consistently carried out on a global scale touching all of the company's key markets, Hyundai used the sponsorship to create an affinity with its consumers.

Brand identity, positioning and personality

Passion branding can be very effective in either establishing or reinforcing a brand's identity, positioning and personality.

Sprite used passion branding to reposition and relaunch itself when the decision was taken by the Coca-Cola Company to align the brand with the NBA in North America as Chuck Fruit explains.

Leading Thought
Chuck Fruit, *Senior Vice President, The Coca-Cola Company*

10 years ago our Sprite brand was a second-tier lemon-lime soft drink that had very little competitive differentiation or unique personality. We used the NBA as the primary platform from which to change the positioning of Sprite to be a very contemporary, hip, urban, beverage brand. The new Sprite positioning had nothing to do with lemon and lime flavours but rather we used NBA players as metaphors for what we wanted the brand personality and proposition to stand for. Sprite sales following that re-positioning and NBA sponsorship grew by double-digit figures for about 6–8 years in a row. It became by far and away the number one brand in its category and the most preferred soft drink for teenagers in the United States.

Another example of where sponsorship is being used to reinforce a brand's identity, personality and image comes from cellular network company Orange who are using their sponsorship of the Orange Prize for Fiction to, amongst other things, characterize Orange's flair and innovation.

CASE STUDY

Orange Prize for Fiction and Orange 'enjoymusic' Tour: entrenching Orange's distinct brand personality through sponsorship

The growth in the number of mobile phone subscribers across the globe has been phenomenal. In 1990 there were a reported 11 million users worldwide and this number is predicted to reach over one billion by 2004.

In this market, Orange has been one of the most successful brand launches of the last decade, despite entering the market well after the likes of the global leader, Vodafone. The reason for their success is that Orange never positioned itself purely as a mobile phone company defined by the mechanics of its market but chose rather to adopt a distinct brand ideology focusing on universal truths that could be translated into action on a global scale. At the time of writing Orange has over 43 million subscribers and has a presence in the UK, France and 9 other countries.

When Orange launched in the UK in April 1994 few thought the brand would shape up against Vodafone and Cellnet's market dominance. Orange was faced with a daunting challenge and needed to have a carefully developed strategy if any impact was to be made.

Orange had a number of important competitive features at the time such as per-second billing, but to adopt a strategy based on 'value for money' would have been detrimental. It would have prevented Orange from taking full advantage of its late entry into the UK market by avoiding the mistakes made by its predecessors. The mobile telephony market had become commoditized and was characterized by confusion and mistrust due to complicated tariffs and price claims.

In order for Orange to make an impact in this sector it was therefore vital to de-emphasize the similarities of its offering, such as cost, and instead create a distinct and strong brand identity and positioning and cultivate a following in this way. The Orange brand vision focused on a 'wirefree future' and the desired brand personality was to be forward-thinking, refreshing, confident, dynamic and always challenging the conventional. This distinct brand vision enabled Orange to distance itself from the vocabulary and associations of the existing telephony market and provided Orange with a sustainable and dynamic source of competitive advantage which engaged consumers on an emotional and rational level and galvanized the organization behind a clear way of communicating and doing business.

No brand ideology is effective unless it is successfully and consistently articulated across all communication channels. Orange adopted a highly successful multimedia advertising schedule which saw the brand achieve higher levels of awareness than either Cellnet or Vodafone after only two years and secured a very potent brand image.

In addition to advertising, sponsorship forms a vital part of Orange's overall communications mix. Orange aligns with various sponsorship properties, using this medium as a powerful differentiator for the brand and a key driver of its distinctive brand personality. In order to remain true to its brand ethos, Orange's sponsorships demonstrate support for the underdog – Orange would never simply align with the biggest or best event or team and use sponsorship primarily as a branding tool. Instead, Orange identifies opportunities where the brand can engage with the consumer and make an impact on a more personal level. Having identified an appropriate sponsorship property, Orange ensures that the distinctive brand personality becomes part and parcel of the property by challenging conventions and doing things differently.

Orange tends to support relatively small, targeted sponsorships outside of the traditional sports environment. Since launch, Orange has become one of Europe's largest corporate sponsors of the arts and leads the way in the UK in terms of innovative arts sponsorships. Orange's flagship sponsorship is undoubtedly the Orange Prize for Fiction, a highly successful literary sponsorship which has grown in stature to become one of Europe's most prestigious literary awards. The Orange enjoymusic Tours form part of Orange's portfolio of music sponsorships targeting the student market.

Orange Prize for Fiction

The Orange Prize for Fiction, which supports excellence and innovation in women's fiction by rewarding the year's best novel by an English-speaking woman, was created in 1996 and was Orange's first major foray into sponsorship. The winner receives a prize of £30,000 and a bronze figurine, the 'Bessie'.

Orange was attracted to the sponsorship platform, not only because, being the first and only award recognizing exclusively female writing, it characterized the flair and innovation associated with the Orange brand but also because it primarily targeted upper-income women, aged 25–45 years who, at the time, were not taking up mobile telephony as quickly as network operators anticipated they would. The subsequent success of the Orange Prize for Fiction, and the educational and life-long learning initiatives run alongside the main award, have ensured that it now reaches a far wider and more diverse audience than initially targeted.

The primary objectives of the sponsorship are as follows:

- Challenge convention and do things differently.
- Use the association to demonstrate the unique and innovative qualities of the Orange brand at a personal level.

True to the Orange personality, the seven year lifespan of the sponsorship has seen a number of innovative marketing and PR programmes that have challenged conventions, ensured the longevity of the sponsorship and kept it in the public eye. In fact, each year Orange makes a point of introducing new, innovative elements that add further depth and interest.

New extensions have included the addition of a shadow men's jury, which sat alongside the official women's jury responsible for selecting the winner, and was aimed at increasing awareness of the Award amongst men. Other new elements introduced over the seven years are *Orange Futures*, a partnership with *Harpers & Queen* magazine aimed at promoting writing by young women writers who potentially could go on to win the Orange Prize for Fiction in future years, and *Orange Chatterbooks*, a scheme run through 120 public libraries in the UK and targeting 4–12 year olds, encouraging them to develop a lifelong love of books. Each group receives a range of reading related materials including reading lists, review notes and games and they get the opportunity to meet authors and illustrators at special events organized by Orange.

In 2003 Orange will be partnering with the Index on Censorship, a group that tackles issues related to freedom of speech and expression. Debates on various issues will be staged at university campuses throughout the UK with the aim of resurrecting the art of debate at universities. This partnership makes perfect sense in that challenging the *status quo* is very much in line with the Orange brand.

At its inception, the Orange Prize for Fiction was ridiculed by the press and opinion makers but in seven years it has evolved, through constant reinvention and reinvestment by Orange, to become a prestigious, highly sought after award with a number of effective extensions. Furthermore, for Orange it is more than just a sponsorship – it is a highly successful campaigning tool that convincingly addresses issues of literacy, education and life-long learning.

The success of the sponsorship is further demonstrated in the following positive impacts on the Orange brand

- Orange has overtaken Vodafone to become the number one mobile phone company in the UK.
- Usage amongst the initial target audience of upper income women, aged 25–45 years has increased.
- In 2001 the sponsorship generated 715 media articles nationally of which 96 per cent were favourable and the total adult audience reached was 42 million people and there was an 18 per cent rise in awareness of the sponsorship, with a 29 per cent rise amongst men.

The above demonstrates clearly how a well-executed non-sport sponsorship can deliver just as effectively as the traditional sports platforms and usually at a fraction of the cost.

Orange enjoymusic Tour

The Orange enjoymusic Tour was created out of a realization that the student market was largely ignored and Orange's desire to be the brand of choice for the youth student market. Students also proved to be the very people who would adopt the emerging data services offered by Orange and would use the services as a cultural social device. The youth student market is however a notoriously cynical and difficult group who are easily turned off by a sponsor shoving its logo at them. The sponsorship property chosen by Orange therefore needed to be highly-targeted and position the brand as a 'peer' in the minds of students in a genuine way whilst still remaining true to the distinct Orange brand personality.

The Orange enjoymusic Tour ran for 40 dates during the academic year, visiting student unions across the United Kingdom. It revolved around the use of cutting-edge music talent that young audiences both expect and demand and, by avoiding superstar DJs, Orange ensured that it remained the 'hero' brand. Campus venues were transformed, using top quality sound and lighting on a par with leading club venues, and indicating Orange's involvement without being too commercially overt as this would only have alienated the target market.

Orange's objectives for the sponsorship were as follows:

- To enhance Orange's reputation as a trusted source of music.
- To reinforce Orange's positioning as a 'lifestyle enabler'.

To maximize the benefits to be gained from the platform, Orange worked closely with the individual college unions and used them to assist in the distribution of posters and flyers to create awareness and excitement around the events. Pre-awareness of the tour was also generated by targeting student press, local press and local radio using pre-recorded shows featuring sets and interviews with the musicians performing on the tour. The student website 'nusonline', which has 350,000 registered users, also proved to be an effective mechanism to generate interest amongst students.

The Tour became a source of conversation and word-of-mouth amongst students created a cult effect where students would travel to other universities to attend the night as well as inform friends at other universities to look out for the Tour in their area. Part of Orange's ethos is to avoid providing cheap giveaways which do nothing for the brand. Instead, during the events, Orange placed space hoppers around the campus, the idea being that students would find these when they left and would pinch them. In this way, Orange gave away a present to attendees but in a way that students would react to and wouldn't expect.

As is the case with all its sponsorships, Orange made every effort to use the enjoymusic Tours to showcase its technologies. Students could play Orange WAP games on giant plasma screens; there were giant text screens for students to send SMS messages to their friends or to the DJs. In addition there were 'Look and Listen' pods which demonstrated the Orange multimedia offering including news alerts from Ananova (which is now owned by Orange). Orange also highlighted its data capture devices by installing a touch-screen kiosk, a 'Video Postcard' pod, from which students could send a 15 second video clip of themselves to their friends via e-mail. This allowed the reach of the event to extend to those not in attendance. Finally, detailed information about Orange products and services was available but there was a strong emphasis away from using a hard-sell approach as this would only have alienated the target audience.

Various other promotional elements were also incorporated as part of the sponsorship. Not only did they add to the overall success of the sponsorship but they also clearly demonstrated Orange's sound understanding of the desires and trigger points amongst students. One such promotion was the 'Free Nights' promotion which addressed the financial realities that face many students by offering colleges one night free-of-charge and thereafter limiting entry charges to a maximum of £4 per entry. The rationale behind this promotion was to give something back in return for the privilege of marketing to this group. Typically student unions have to pay exorbitant amounts to host similar type functions and the cost is transferred to students through expensive ticket prices. By providing the enjoymusic Tour free to the student unions, Orange allowed the student unions to keep ticket prices to a minimum and to invest more money in the universities.

A fun element that created interactivity with the target market was the Glow Wall whereby students could capture their own shadow on the glow

Figure 3.3 Orange giant plasma screens. Reprinted with permission from Orange

wall by striking a pose which then triggered a strobe light. When students walked away their image remained. There were also roving cameras which captured students enjoying themselves at the events. This in turn drove traffic to the Orange website as students were encouraged to go to the website to see if their picture was displayed in the 'Rogues Gallery.'

The Orange enjoymusic Tour proved to be highly successful as a sponsorship platform aiming to reach and influence the student target market.

- 45,000 students attended the Tour, with 65 per cent of them saying that it provided genuine value for money and a further 90 per cent saying they would attend the event again.
- Over 80 per cent of the total UK student market were aware of the Orange enjoymusic Tour events.
- PR coverage was estimated to be valued at £2.2 million.
- More importantly, the positive effect of the sponsorship is evident in Orange's market share amongst students which rose from 26 per cent to 34 per cent during the course of the programme.

Denise Lewis, Group Director of Corporate Affairs and Sponsorship at Orange, sums up Orange's successful approach to sponsorship succinctly:

Figure 3.4 Orange 'look and listen' pods. Reprinted with permission from Orange

In the short period since our launch, we have built a sponsorship portfolio which is radically different from traditional sponsorship practises as well as from the activity of our many competitors.

Our approach has been to be a key differentiator in the whole area of marketing and brand communications and a key driver in influencing consumer perceptions of our brand, vision and values. Throughout, we have sought to build a portfolio based on doing things differently, challenging conventions, stimulating debate, investing in the future and enabling things to happen.

We have never viewed sponsorship as a mere badging exercise nor have we ever tried to associate ourselves with the biggest or the best. Rather, we have used it as a sophisticated platform from which to personally engage with our customers and in our view, thereby enhance their experience of and loyalty to, Orange.

Since our launch, in what is only a very brief period of time, our sponsorship work has been recognized universally. We have become Europe's number one corporate sponsor of the arts winning many awards: 3 consecutive Hollis Awards, the Financial Times *Best European Corporate Sponsor and most recently the ESCA (European Sponsorship Consultants Association) – European Sponsor of the Year Award.*

As always, the future is bright, the future is Orange.

KEY INSIGHT

By choosing non-traditional passion branding platforms with no clutter a brand is able to stand out and set itself apart from other brands in its product sector. A clear brand vision and identity allows brands to select and utilize sponsorship opportunities that become a credible manifestation and extension of the brand, and which can be fully integrated across the business and thereby achieve excellent results. Furthermore, through its sponsorships, Orange also proves that, provided a brand has a strong image, high awareness figures can be created without overt use of the company logo.

Brand differentiation

In a world of product and service parity, opportunities to differentiate one company and/or brand from another are much sought after.

As a result of the principle of 'category exclusivity' whereby competing products and services are excluded from any association with a passion platform, passion branding provides just such an opportunity.

A passion branding campaign can be used to differentiate a company or brand from its competitors using the direct association with the passion platform and the extensions that flow from this association as the point of difference.

So, for example, in the financial services category where there is in truth very little difference between the products and services provided by competing financial institutions, an exclusive association by Bank A with passion platform B can be used as a major point of differentiation.

A great example of this is found in South Africa through Nedbank's Affinity Programme which not only proved to be hugely effective in differentiating Nedbank from its competitors in what is a very competitive environment but also ended up being a major driver of incremental business for the bank.

CASE STUDY

Nedbank Arts, Green and Sport

The financial services sector is notoriously competitive but also lacks strong brand differentiation. Customers are generally somewhat cynical towards banks, believing them to offer little by way of genuine added-value and good customer service. Nedbank, one of South Africa's leading retail banking institutions, carried out research in the late 1980s which showed that, whilst customers wanted good service and competitive product offerings, they also wanted their bank to project a softer, more caring attitude.

Bearing this in mind, Nedbank embarked on a cause-related, or mutual benefit, marketing drive in the form of Nedbank Arts, Green and Sport – formerly known as Nedbank Affinities. This created a strongly differentiated offering for the bank in a parity market. The aim of Nedbank Arts, Green and Sport was to build brand differentiation and loyalty by linking cheque books, credit cards and savings accounts to an emotional commitment or cause thereby growing Nedbank's client base, fostering increased loyalty among existing clients and ultimately improving market share.

Nedbank Arts, Green and Sport supports three trusts – The Green Trust, the Arts & Culture Trust and The Sports Trust – which are the vehicles through which Nedbank clients can contribute towards the social capital of the country. Clients choose which trust, or combination of trusts, they would like to support, according to their personal interests, and their use of Nedbank Arts, Green or Sport banking products funds the trusts in the following ways:

- A percentage of annual turnover on credit cards is donated to the relevant trust, at no cost to the client.
- A R9 premium, paid by the client, is donated for each new chequebook issued.

- A R2.50 donation for each new savings account opened is donated by Nedbank to the trust, again at no client cost.

It should be noted that using Nedbank Arts, Green or Sport banking products incurs no additional cost to clients – all service fees are exactly the same as for regular Nedbank products. Instead, Nedbank donates funds to the relevant trust on behalf of its Nedbank Arts, Green and Sport clients – so the clients do not pay anything. The only exception to this is that Nedbank Arts, Green and Sport clients pay a small premium for each new chequebook ordered – and this premium is donated directly to the trust concerned.

The Green Trust was launched by Nedbank and WWF-SA, the conservation organization, in 1990. Following on from the success of The Green Trust, The Sports Trust and the Arts & Culture Trust were launched in 1994, with Nedbank as the initiator and a founder member of both trusts. The Arts & Culture Trust encompasses all genres of arts and culture, from theatre to photography to arts education, and supports four broad areas of activity – skills training and education in the arts; the development of a cultural infrastructure; the production and dissemination of creative work and audience development. The Sports Trust focuses on the allocation of funds in two main areas – the building of sports facilities (physical resources) and human resources, which includes the identification of young sporting talent, coaching and training.

A range of event sponsorships is linked to Nedbank Arts, Green and Sport, carefully chosen to maximize exposure in the marketplace and build brand loyalty and top-of-mind awareness. Nedbank views these sponsorships as operating on the principle of catalytic marketing, where the promotion of a particular event cascades into support for the Nedbank brand and the use of its products.

The success of the Nedbank Arts, Green and Sport can be illustrated on a number of levels:

- The Affinities have definitely created a powerful bond of identification between the client and bank and have helped to build a warmer, softer image of Nedbank.
  Of the four main banks, research shows that Nedbank scores highest on

the 'softer banking' variable, and 83 per cent of committed clients stated 'cares about the environment' as a factor driving their commitment to Nedbank.

- Nedbank research indicates that client retention (loyalty) is substantially higher for Affinity-linked account holders compared to generic account holders. The average life of an Affinity account is roughly double that of a generic account.

- The Green Trust Affinity has been Nedbank's most successful product – approximately 75 per cent of all product generated funds are channelled to the Green Trust. In addition Nedbank has received international recognition for the Green Trust in the form of the WWF's Golden Panda Award in recognition of the bank's role in helping to protect and improve the environment.

KEY INSIGHT

In order for a point difference to enhance the brand truly, it must address a consumer need and offer them something they can relate to and that they desire. By researching their clients before creating Nedbank Arts, Green and Sport, Nedbank was able to develop lifestyle portfolios that address the needs of its target market and thereby help to create a greater affinity between Nedbank and its clients.

Leading Thought
Sean O'Neill, *Brand and Market Communication Director, Diageo*

I truly believe that better results come from greater focus. I am not a believer of creating a large number of objectives against a particular sponsorship – not least because we know that sponsorship cannot deliver everything. Clarity is paramount.

This was one of the great learnings from Rugby World Cup in '99. Here we were faced with different markets each with different challenges and with different consumers, and we tried to get our sponsorship to deliver against a great many things – incremental volume, greater affinity, stronger image, new drinkers, awareness. We weren't truly focused enough – and against some of the objectives, this showed.

That said, there's a number of levels on which sponsorship can help drive brand growth. One of these is leveraging an association over time to reflect what we call the key brand benefit. Take Johnnie Walker which has at its heart the concept and philosophy of personal progress. Selecting a sponsorship over time, which motivates consumers to have goals and dreams and to then pursue and achieve them would be a significant way of building affinity and consideration for the brand.

Sponsorship has a really important role in bringing the key brand benefit to life because for me, it's the one discipline that can really engage and involve the consumer in something that is a passion for them. Through sponsorship you can get a total brand experience through using the property as a base for advertising, promotions, hospitality, PR etc. Added to this, (aside from broadcast sponsorships) consumers can literally touch, feel and see the entity with which you're associated.

An example of this would be the Johnnie Walker Classic which is one of the premier golf tournaments in the European tour. We've run that for 12 years yet we are absolutely clear that it is not so much a golf event as a brand event for us. Of course, we never get away from the fact that you need to deliver a great golf tournament, but its paramount that through our exploitation there needs to be a consistent brand message which brings the key brand benefit to life and which finds a way of deepening consumers' understanding of what that means.

KEY INSIGHT

Passion branding can provide invaluable opportunities for a brand to draw on the fans' real life experiences and in the process positively shape the consumers' attitudes towards, and perception of, the brand. The benefits of passion branding for enhancing brand equity can potentially include the following:

- *Brand loyalty – positive effect on purchasing behaviour.*
- *Brand awareness – consumer attention.*
- *Brand attributes and benefits – first hand experience.*
- *Brand associations – value exchange with the platform and its sponsors.*
- *Brand identity, positioning and personality – real life examples.*
- *Brand differentiation – competitive advantage.*

4

Passion branding – more than just brand building

Passion branding provides a number of other invaluable opportunities for a truly integrated communications campaign. Traditional media are often limited in their ability to be effective in more than one area at a time and often have an effect on one area at the expense of another. A sales promotion, for example, may bring about a peak in revenue for a brief period but often at the expense of brand equity. Passion branding is unique in its ability to both build strong brands while at the same time increasing revenue as well as achieving a number of other objectives.

Driving revenue growth

Increasingly, marketers should be looking to their passion branding activities to maintain or increase revenues, either directly or indirectly.

The ability of passion branding to achieve such an objective does however vary from category to category. So, for example, revenue opportunities within the financial services category may not be as obvious as say those within the fast-moving consumer goods (FMCG) category. However, with an open and creative mind, there should be no reason why passion branding cannot contribute to a business in this way.

Direct Sales

In every passion branding campaign, opportunities will exist to drive incremental revenues through the sale of products and services to the fans themselves either at the venue or through other media consumed by the fans.

If it is a soft drink that you are selling, then the 60,000 fans at the game will present the perfect captive target audience. As a sponsor of the event, the soft drink brand will not only be able to drive incremental sales but it will also be able to shut out its competitors. Equally, a sales promotion linked directly to a passion branding campaign can also make a positive contribution to direct sales.

If you are a cell phone operator for instance, then a call-in phone competition connected to the sponsorship will provide a great opportunity to generate call revenue whilst demonstrating the efficiency of the network. Likewise, a promotion aimed at getting fans to SMS their man of the match will provide both an element of interactivity as well as revenue generation.

Leading Thought

Lawrence Flanagan, *Executive Vice President and Chief Marketing Officer for Global Marketing, MasterCard International*

All of our integrated marketing programmes are developed to drive revenue. Sponsorships are one of the channels that we use to achieve this. As such, we hold sponsorships to the same level of accountability as we do every other marketing programme that we have.

When you step back and look at how sponsorship is being used generally both within the financial community and outside it, I would say that there is a lot of wastage going on. Even with MasterCard in the earlier days, we were putting up logos on boards or saying 'the official card of' or 'beloved fan of' which looking back was a waste of money.

It's really only over the past 5 years or so that we've had this global brand positioning, this very effective 'Priceless' campaign, this new language to speak to consumers, that we've really been able to make World Cup and other sponsorships really deliver against our objectives and deliver real value for us. This is because we're not just managing our sponsorships as stand alone activities, an off-shoot of our marketing programme, but rather because sponsorship is integrated with everything else we do.

Indirect Sales

The added value of sponsorship comes through when you identify ways in which your passion branding campaign can be used to influence sales within a wider market beyond those directly targeted through the passion platform itself. In such instances, the sponsorship can be used as leverage to secure distribution channels that might otherwise not be available to the marketer.

Leading Thought
Chuck Fruit, *Senior Vice President, The Coca-Cola Company*

We use sponsorship as a business builder in terms of facilitating direct commerce, opening up new retail customers for us.

Some sponsorships lend themselves to driving sales more readily than others. My favourite case study is NASCAR here in the United States where we were able to document the profitable return on our sponsorship investment. As a result of our increased involvement in NASCAR and our interaction with other NASCAR sponsors, we got to know several other companies who were big NASCAR sponsors and with whom we had no prior business relationship.

The NAPA auto parts chain is one such example where our NASCAR relationship opened up opportunities for us to sell Coca-Cola in every one of their stores across the country. Likewise, Home Depot, the giant home improvement chain, is a big NASCAR sponsor. NASCAR sponsorship opened up opportunities for us to get availability in all of their stores. And we were able to get increased promotional display opportunities with a couple of major grocery chains who were very enthused with our NASCAR association. Just from that new distribution and increased in-store display activity, we were able to document that our entire NASCAR investment paid off, forgetting the brand building and the consumer benefits.

Another example that makes a compelling case for the sales potential of passion branding comes from MTN, a leading mobile (cell) phone network operator in South Africa, and its sponsorship of the MTN Gladiators television entertainment show.

CASE STUDY

MTN Gladiators: Using sponsorship to drive revenue growth

The mobile telephony market in South Africa is highly competitive, as it is anywhere else in the world. The South African market is dominated by two major players, Vodacom, the market leader by a small margin, and Mobile Telephone Networks (MTN). A third service provider, Cell C, has also recently entered the market and is making inroads as well.

In 1998, Vodacom was significantly outspending MTN in terms of marketing in order to support its positioning as South Africa's 'leading cellular network.' MTN needed to find a suitable means by which to challenge this positioning and identified sponsorship as a way in which to do this. Since sport sponsorship was becoming increasingly cluttered and expensive, MTN chose something completely different and took on the sponsorship of the Gladiators, a property which allowed MTN to dominate the environment as the sole sponsor aligned with the property. MTN Gladiators proved to be the ideal platform to appeal to a broad target audience and off which to drive the key MTN brand attributes of 'fun' and 'family minded', not to mention the revenue generating opportunities that the sponsorship created.

The sponsorship was centred around the weekly MTN Gladiators television show which saw costumed gladiators pit their formidable skills against challengers in an arena littered with obstacles. In order to maximize the benefits created by the association with the Gladiators, MTN integrated the sponsorship across a number of additional channels including advertising, sales promotions, eventing and special appearances by the MTN Gladiator personalities as well as licensing and merchandising.

The objectives of the sponsorship were:

• To generate high levels of brand awareness and likeability, primarily through the media.
• To use the popularity of the MTN Gladiators to support MTN's business objectives in terms of retention, acquisition and revenue generation.

Brand presence was created through the naming rights to the broadcast sponsorship, a comprehensive media PR campaign, extensive use of the MTN Gladiators logo in a multi-media approach and through the licensing and merchandizing programme. The success of the M&L programme was evident in a deal which was concluded with the South African Post Office whereby an MTN Gladiators range of stamps was produced. This was the first time that a commercial brand had appeared on a local stamp and over 4 million stamps were sold. In addition MTN negotiated a deal with the fast food chain, Wimpy, for a month long licensed promotion which resulted in 350,000 additional logo impressions for MTN Gladiators and Wimpy's best grossing month ever. Based on the success of this initial promotion, Wimpy has since developed other MTN Gladiators themed promotions all of which have been highly successful.

Likeability was enhanced through experiential opportunities which saw the Gladiator personalities conduct various roadshows and appearances around the country.

Staff were also made to feel part of the sponsorship through regular communication, free tickets to the shows and opportunities for one-on-one interaction with the Gladiator personalities.

Revenue generation involved a two-pronged approach aimed at acquiring new subscribers and retaining existing ones. The acquisition strategy saw the launch of two new Gladiator-themed cellular offerings and the use of merchandizing and licensing items as added value to entice new subscribers. In order to encourage retention of existing customers and drive registrations for Call Awards, MTN's subscriber loyalty programme, MTN offered exclusive benefits such as preferential booking to attend the MTN Gladiator shows, opportunities to meet the Gladiator personalities, VIP subscriber packages to customers and Gladiator ring tones and logos.

In terms of untapping additional revenue opportunities, MTN lines were used for ticket sales and, even more impactful was the way in which MTN

Figure 4.1 Gladiators in Combat. Reprinted with permission from Mobile Telephone Networks

Figure 4.2 Gladiator Challenges. Reprinted with permission from Mobile Telephone Networks

used its alignment with the popular Gladiators to secure additional distribution channels. Two leading national chain stores were secured as distribution channels in this way.

Evaluating the results of the MTN Gladiators sponsorship emphasizes just how successful the sponsorship was for the brand in terms of the two objectives it set out to achieve.

In terms of brand presence alone, television exposure was valued at one and a half times the amount paid for the broadcast package and PR exposure was double the target set. In addition 5 million logo impressions were created through the media and through the various licensing and merchandizing initiatives. Spontaneous awareness of the sponsorship was 55 per cent amongst the national adult population thus making it one of the most recognizable sponsorships in South Africa.

Internally, MTN staff were overwhelmingly in favour of the sponsorship with 78 per cent indicating that they like to watch the show on television.

In terms of revenue generation, the total amount generated directly as a result of the show amounted to R6.9 million (through use of the MTN lines, ring tones etc). In addition, MTN Gladiators resulted in a 6 per cent increase in Call Awards registration. Of course all of this excludes the longer term and more substantial benefits which have accrued as a result of securing the two additional distribution channels.

All in all MTN's association with the Gladiators was an enormous success. As sheer entertainment value, it certainly proved its worth and as a sponsorship investment it showed a return on investment that was almost five times the total sponsorship cost. Furthermore, it proved that sponsorship can have a direct and significant impact on sales provided it is leveraged effectively.

KEY INSIGHT

Extend the value of the sponsorship by exploring all possible areas where it can be leveraged and where it can generate revenue directly for the brand. Capitalize on the value that consumers attach to the brand being sponsored and convert this value into value for the sponsoring brand in terms of a more positive perception of the brand and increased sales.

Creating the appropriate environment

It is also relevant to consider whether it is realistic to assume that passion branding can do a sales job for a brand. This is particularly the case in certain categories, like life assurance, where the product is more 'sold' than it is 'bought' by consumers and the role that passion branding plays in the sale is more connected to creating the appropriate environment in which the sale can be made.

Related new revenue sources

Passion branding has the ability to tap additional revenue sources that can be used to contribute towards the costs of the campaign. This potential will to a large extent depend on the relationship between the passion brander and the promoter as well as the risk appetite of the former.

Where a passion brander has both the opportunity and the desire, one such example is that of the sale of licensed products linked to the sponsorship. Where the fan base is large enough, the opportunity may exist to license the passion brand marks into all forms of merchandise –

clothing, crockery, posters, and so on – as was demonstrated by MTN with its Gladiators sponsorship. In the process, and assuming that you read the market right, the potential exists to generate incremental funding that can in the right circumstances be very material.

Another great example of this comes from Peter Stuyvesant who, a number of years ago in South Africa, decided to use sponsorship of music spectaculars as a marketing platform. Rather than simply sponsor music concerts with leading acts like Tina Turner, Michael Jackson and the like, Peter Stuyvesant took the position of promoter for the events. In so doing, Peter Stuyvesant ultimately ended up with a self-funding promotion that did an awesome job for the brand. Yes, a high-risk approach but one that paid off handsomely thanks to the professionalism of the people at Peter Stuyvesant that drove and managed the project.

Energizing staff

If set as an objective, passion branding has the ability to positively influence staff morale and in the process efficiency and effectiveness. In fact, employees are increasingly expecting it of their employers that they do more than just pay their salaries.

This factor is highlighted in the 2001 Cone/Roper Corporate Citizenship Study which indicates that the majority of American employees expect their employers to play an active role in supporting social needs. Post September 11, 83 per cent of Americans believe it is more important than ever for the companies they work for to support the needs of society. The report goes on to indicate that a company can have a positive impact on employee morale through such involvement with 38 per cent of employees whose companies have cause related programmes saying that they are more likely to say they are proud of their company's values than company employees who do not have such programmes.

What this confirms therefore is that a company's passion branding activities can be used to nurture employee relationships while at the same time doing the same for consumer relationships.

The most effective employee-focused efforts that I have witnessed have been those that provide employees with the opportunity to become actively involved in the passion branding campaign as opposed to being passive bystanders. In the process, not only is good achieved for the company as its staff become its active ambassadors but a sense of self-achievement results which has strong psychological benefits for the employees themselves.

One such example is evident in the Proudly South African Campaign which is detailed as a case study in Chapter 5. The campaign's main focus is to create jobs by promoting South African products and services. Companies who fulfil the four requirements, namely a minimum 50 per cent local production, fair labour and environmental practice and a commitment to quality, can become members of the campaign.

As part of the marketing campaign, a Proudly South African Day was initiated whereby member companies were encouraged to demonstrate their commitment. On 23rd September 2002, Proudly South African Day, staff from companies all over South Africa came out to actively support the campaign and celebrate their South African heritage in any number of ways ranging from dressing to a Proudly South African theme, creating a Proudly South African poem, song, meal or cocktail to decorating their offices in a way that reflected their Proudly South African member status. On a more serious note, staff were incentivized to recruit additional member companies and to steer their purchasing habits towards buying local products that display the Proudly South African logo. Prizes were awarded to companies who demonstrated the most support across six different categories. The campaign was well supported by many of Proudly South African's 400 member companies and created much goodwill amongst participating staff.

Motivating the trade

A major component of any consumer-oriented business is the extent to which a brand enjoys the support of the trade.

Passion branding can play a major role in assisting with the nurturing of relationships with the trade by, for example, using hospitality linked incentives where the trade are incentivized to support the sponsoring brand in return for the opportunity to attend a major sponsored event.

J&B Whisky, as an example, use this approach very successfully around their sponsorship of the J&B Met, one of South Africa's leading social events that happens in Cape Town in February each year and has grown to become J&B's biggest sponsorship worldwide. An invitation to the J&B VIP Marquee on J&B Met day, an exclusive hospitality offering, is much sought after and proves to be a valuable incentive that the J&B sales team puts to good use in ensuring relationships with the trade are strengthened.

Experiential marketing

Although not automatically the case, event-oriented passion branding campaigns provide wonderful opportunities for a brand to provide consumers with a unique brand experience in which the brand's core essence, identity and benefits are brought to life – can be touched and felt.

This is particularly the case where a brand has, by nature of the category in which it exists, limited opportunities to interact with the consumer in an experiential way. A good example would be a short-term insurance brand in which the brand/consumer interface is typically limited by the grudge nature of the purchase of such products. Such a brand could use the experiential capacity of an event to demonstrate its brand attributes and values in a way that would not have any of the negative connotations normally associated with an interface between the brand and its customers.

While traditional advertising may be regarded as one way selling, passion branding is about two-way communication. The experiences that passion branding can involve consumers in can be invaluable in shaping attitudes towards a brand.

Coca-Cola have become very effective over the years in layering a unique added value Coca-Cola fan experience around the passion platforms that they associate with. I witnessed this first-hand at the 1996 Atlanta Olympic Games where Coca-Cola went out of their way to make sure that the Olympic fans enjoyment of the Games was enhanced. This included things like a Coca-Cola cool-off area that the fans could walk through to escape from the intense heat in Atlanta at the time of the Games and a Coca-Cola Fan Village in which fans could experience first-hand some of the special things about the Games, e.g., how high the world record for the high jump really was, what it might feel like to race against Michael Johnson in the 100 m and so on.

The great thing about passion branding-linked brand experiences is that they enhance the fans' enjoyment and consumption of their passion and in the process really position the sponsoring brand as part and parcel of the fans' passion. The credibility that flows to the sponsoring brand as a result of this commitment can be invaluable.

Leading Thought
Chuck Fruit, *Senior Vice President, The Coca-Cola Company*

We view sponsorship as an extension of our overall marketing strategy about brand presence and ubiquity. So we want Coca-Cola to be present wherever people are having good times with family and friends. But we learned over the years, particularly as there became more sponsorship competition, that being there was not enough. Coca-Cola had to make a difference in the experience for the fan. That's really what drove our focus on fan experience . . . and maybe less of an emphasis on passive signage and presence.

We also learned that you need to understand what the fan's passion really is in that environment and what your brand's role can be in enhancing that passion. And certainly the role of Coca-Cola is going to be dramatically different than a role of an automotive or a financial services company.

We believe therefore that the crux of sponsorship today is understanding the fans, identifying the sweet spot in terms of their passion and the brand's appropriate role in that passion, and then delivering on it.

A sponsor does one of three things. They're either *invisible* to the consumer, which is probably the case in most sponsorships. They can *detract* from the consumer's experience through 'over-commercialization' or by throwing big logos over places where the consumer wishes there weren't any logos; or, in a few cases, they can actually *enhance* the fan's experience through relevant, entertaining, engaging advertising or by actually enhancing the fan's fun and enjoyment at the event.

For example, we want Coca-Cola to have a direct relationship with football fans based on their passion. I think we can tailor our sponsorship programs and benefits to them based on their specific interests and passions. We really haven't done this yet, but this is a huge opportunity.

For Coca-Cola, therefore, I think it's all going to be about 'personal relationships' with the fans and enhancing the fans' enjoyment with their sports passions. We don't yet know how to do this precisely, but I think we know the space we should be playing in.

Sponsor/Sponsee partnerships

The relationship between sponsors and sponsees has potential benefits for both parties. The most successful relationships are those where the approach is one of a true partnership with both the sponsor and sponsee recognizing the contribution that each can make to the other's brand and business in general.

As in all things in life, the sustainability of any relationship depends on the extent to which that relationship is mutually beneficial or 'win-win' to all parties. A healthy property is good for a sponsor just as a healthy sponsor is good for a property.

Sponsors therefore have the opportunity to not only build their own brands and drive their own bottom line through their sponsorships but also the opportunity to contribute towards the growth of the sponsored property's brand and financial independence.

Sponsees also have a role to play in helping their sponsors achieve their brand and business objectives. As custodians of their fans' passion, sponsees can play a major role in helping their sponsors to harness the power of this passion in a positive way.

Leading Thought
Patrick Magyar, *Chief Executive Officer, FIFA Marketing AG*

We are one of the first large bodies and events that really have understood that sports marketing is about much more than just the money. It is about developing a business partnership with our sponsors who leverage the long-term equity of our event through their advertising and PR and public relations efforts. Equally, we need to be in the business of helping them to reach their targets according to their marketing strategy. Ultimately, this results in them selling more Coke, more hamburgers, more TVs. We don't want to over commercialize our event but rather, together with our sponsors, build solid business opportunities from which we all ultimately benefit.

5

Passion platforms

A number of potential passion assets or passion platforms exist – it is up to the marketer to decide which will provide the most fertile ground for achieving the business and communication objectives identified for the brand. Getting this right is crucial to the success of an effective passion branding campaign and, after having identified if indeed passion branding does have a role to play as part of a brand's marketing and communications mix, it is probably the most important decision to be made by a passion brander.

The decision as to which type of passion platform is most appropriate will be informed first and foremost by an understanding of the platform's fans. After that, the fit or relevance between the platform's fans and your brand's consumers, both demographically and attitudinally, and your brand's business and communication objectives, can be assessed.

For ease of reference, I've classified the various passion platforms into the following broad categories:

- Sports and entertainment marketing.
- Cause related Marketing.
- Social responsibility marketing.
- Public/private sector partnerships.
- Public domain marketing.

Irrespective of the platform that eventually ends up on the drawing-board, the rules of engagement are much the same.

Each platform provides an opportunity to develop a relationship with consumers in an environment of their choice, one where they will have invited you in to their space and given you permission to talk to them in an environment where they are likely to be more receptive to your messages in recognition of the value that you are adding to their relationship with and around their passion.

Sport and entertainment marketing

Definition of sport and entertainment marketing

Sport and entertainment marketing involves the association of a brand with a marketing asset, e.g.: a sports event, and the leverage of that association by a sponsor in order to positively impact brand image and/or sales.

Sport – king of the mix

Since the early 1960s when Mark McCormack first identified the marketing potential to brands of associating themselves with golfing greats Jack Nicklaus, Arnold Palmer and Gary Player, sport has played the dominant role in the sponsorship mix. According to SportBusiness, of the US$2.2 billion that was spent on sponsorship rights globally in 2001, 68 per cent was spent on sports' rights, 17 per cent on broadcast sponsorships, 6 per cent on arts and culture and the balance on causes.

Marketing assets

Sport – soccer to bog snorkelling

There are well over 200 different sporting categories to choose from, ranging from the established giants like soccer and Formula One that boast followers in the billions to the small niche sports like Jukskei (yes, there is such a thing!) that would be lucky to claim more than a few hundred supporters.

Table 5.1 Top sponsored sports in number of deals January–December 2001. Reprinted with permission from Sports Marketing Surveys Ltd.

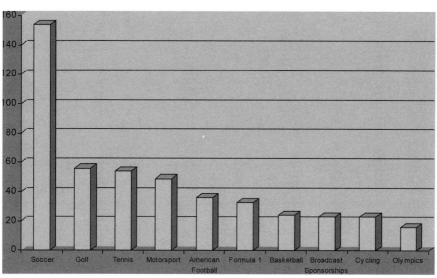

A recent phenomenon is that of extreme and adventure sports with major events like Gravity Games and X Games moving from left field to centre stage as these sports start to become part of popular culture, particularly in North America.

Leading Thought
Michael Payne, *Marketing Director, International Olympic Committee*

The power of passion is what makes sports marketing and sports sponsorship potentially such a valuable tool to a marketer. The ability of sports sponsorship to engage the consumer on something that they care about and, as a result, to be able to stand out from your competitors, is what everybody is fighting for. Sport, and to a certain extent music, are the two vehicles that can provide that connection to your consumers that other forms of marketing do less effectively.

As a sports property therefore you've got to remember ultimately who your client base is, and that is the sports fans, the spectators. You ignore them and you'll suffer – as any marketer would to ignore their consumers.

Table 5.2 Top sponsored sports in value committed Jan–Dec 2001 (US$'000m). Reprinted with permission from Sports Marketing Surveys, Ltd

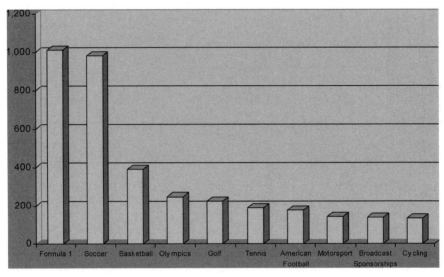

Entertainment – music to festivals

As sport becomes more and more cluttered, expensive and increasingly more difficult to stand out in, marketers are increasingly looking towards other entertainment genres to replace their sports platforms – music, theatre, dance, art and the like. These all offer tremendously exciting opportunities for savvy passion branders, in an environment that can be less structured and formal than is usually the case in sport and therefore present greater opportunities for creativity and innovation.

Leading Thought
Iain Banner, *Chief Executive, Laureus World Sports Awards*

In South Africa we developed the Peter Stuyvesant Music Spectaculars concept. It was very interesting to take the medium of music, which no marketer had really harnessed, and saying 'Right, how do we create ownership of the medium?' – taking a big established brand, a brand that needed to remain relevant and international and using music as a communication form. The association of the brand with the greatest names in world music worked – it became the platform for above-, below- and through-the-line communication.

Basically it was about retaining existing consumers. It was about keeping the brand international and aspirational and keeping the competition out rather than trying to grow market share – although the brand continued to grow through that time.

Music and sport are, as we know, very powerful mediums now. The challenges will come from the next generation as today's children start entering the market... we've seen it already, a kind of new wave of informed consumers that is motivated by different factors to those we treat as commonplace today.

What is also driving passion branders in search of these new platforms is the realization that in a changing world, traditional sport may no longer have the same relevance to Generation X and Y that it does to the affluent baby boomer market. This really struck home for me recently when presenting my thoughts on passion branding to a group of 18–24 year old students at Ogilvy & Mather's Red and Yellow School of advertising.

When asked to split themselves into groups of like-minded passions, it was fascinating to see that only four students from a group of over 40 opted to nominate sports as their primary passion. Interestingly enough sex, alcohol, music, dance and socializing with friends came out tops with more than two thirds of the class nominating these areas of interest as their primary passion.

Do not assume anything in the passion economy. Make a point of understanding what it is that your target consumers are passionate about before embarking on any passion branding campaign.

Leading Thought
Chris Weil, *Chairman and Chief Executive, Momentum Worldwide*

For the launch of Amex Blue Card we were trying to reach a younger audience than Amex had traditionally targeted. Amex was known for theatre and Broadway and the symphony – all very relevant to its target audience.

We said that, if we want to really get the message out there that something is different about Blue Card, we have to come out doing things completely unexpected. So we came up with a music sponsorship platform where we started by creating an event in Central Park, the first ever live trimulcast from Central Park, which we broadcast live on network television, syndicated on a 150 radio stations and screened live on the internet. We had Sheryl Crow, Eric Clapton, Stevie Nicks, Dixie Chicks, Keith Richards from the Stones, Chrissie Hind.

To get tickets to the event we went out and signed people up for the Blue Card all around New York and had an instant win game so people were signing up, getting to win tickets and then we took it from there. We did sponsorship of all of the outdoor arenas around the US, we had a CD that was made out of the Central Park show and the CD, when you opened it, had an application for the Blue Card. The CD went on to be nominated for 3 Grammys and won a Grammy. So it was one of those that the artist did well out of it, and we actually kept part of the proceeds for the sale of the CD – the artist did well, the company did well and the music still continues. You can go on the Blue for Music website and there are still ties back to retail and ticket access and things like that, so it's been a stable platform for Blue since it launched.

A wide range of associations – people to stadiums

Within each sporting and entertainment category there exists the opportunity to sponsor an event, a team, an athlete, a broadcast, a stadium and various other elements within the category.

Event Sponsorship

The primary relationship is between the sponsoring brand and the rights owners/organizers of the event, often facilitated by an intermediary sponsorship agency or the owners in-house sponsorship department.

Rights available around an event usually range from naming rights, e.g., Flora London Marathon, to presenting rights, e.g., Nelson Mandela Invitational presented by PricewaterhouseCoopers, to official supplier rights, e.g., Powerade, Official Supplier to the Stormers.

Each level of sponsorship brings with it a certain level of rights or benefits that are 'sold' to the sponsoring brand in return for a rights fee.

Team Sponsorship

The primary relationship is between the sponsoring brand and the team owners.

Rights available range from shirt sponsor, e.g., Vodafone and Manchester United Football Club, the equivalent of a title sponsorship to an event where, amongst other rights, the sponsor's name and/or logo would be included on the players' shirts, through to official team sponsors and suppliers.

The availability of such sponsorships will vary from sport to sport and from country to country. For example, as prevalent as shirt sponsorships may be in soccer they are non-existent in professional American sports like basketball and baseball.

CASE STUDY

NTL's sponsorship of the British Lions: how NTL used its Lions Team sponsorship to create awareness of the company's products and services, unite its diverse divisions and build staff morale

Although relatively new, NTL was a well-established company in Europe by 2001 with prompted brand-awareness of close to 80 per cent and yet only a third of NTL's prospective customers actually knew that the company supplied telephone, TV, internet and broadband services. The challenge for NTL was therefore to find an effective way to communicate with prospective customers and inform them of the company's diverse product offerings.

NTL elected to take up sponsorship of the Lions team on its tour to Australia in 2001 and to use this as the vehicle through which to drive the necessary messages to customers. The property provided the desired fit for various reasons. Firstly, there was strong synergy between the values of the Lions and the NTL brand in that both inspired passion and inspiration, representing the pinnacle of their respective fields. Secondly, there was also a strong geographical fit in that all four of the home nations making up the Lions team represented key markets for NTL which was crucial if NTL was to effectively use the sponsorship to generate awareness of its offerings amongst the right target audience. Thirdly, rugby represented a trusted medium with a solid supporter base amongst high-income males who are a significant portion of NTL's current and prospective customer base.

NTL's sponsorship objectives were as follows:

- Raise NTL spontaneous brand awareness among high income (ABC1) males to over 25 per cent.
- Deliver a media value of £1.2 million (valued at 30 per cent of rate card).
- Raise NTL product awareness – especially broadband.
- Take ownership of the Tour.
- Deliver viable showcasing for product via an internet site, exclusive TV channel, interactive TV and cut-price telephone calls.
- Use the sponsorship to unite the diverse divisions of NTL and build internal pride and morale among employees.

Key to the success of the sponsorship were the rights that NTL negotiated in order for the company to build a tailored campaign that delivered against the stated objectives. NTL negotiated shirt-branding, using a colour logo for the first time on a Lions' shirt, 50 per cent of all other signage, 37 player appearances, 1 full squad appearance, website rights and exclusive behind-the-scenes access which provided exclusive content that could be used to drive customers to NTL products on TV and the internet during the Tour.

The sponsorship was leveraged pre the Tour on a number of levels, integrating a consistent message across all elements. A national print, television and outdoor advertising campaign was created using the theme 'Up Close and Personal' and highlighting the behind-the-scenes access and depth of exclusive content that NTL could offer the rugby fan during the Tour. NTL also sponsored a supplement in the UK's *Sunday Times* which was considered to be the comprehensive guide to the Tour. In addition, NTL bought title sponsorship of exclusive radio access to referee's comments during Six Nations rugby matches at Twickenham which again delivered the message of 'Up Close and Personal' during the build up to the Tour.

A micro-site (NTL.com/lions) was launched to give fans the opportunity to gain exclusive access to 'Diary of a Lion' during the Tour. The site also included a daily one-minute video clip of behind-the-scenes footage of the Tour, a fantasy Lions game and an interactive message board giving fans the opportunity to communicate with players on the Tour.

NTL also created an exclusive Lions Tour TV channel for NTL customers. This was placed next to Sky Sports to capture channel hoppers and featured a 24-hour looped showreel of NTL's exclusive behind-the-scenes footage.

To support the above-the-line activities, NTL initiated a pre- and on-Tour PR campaign which pushed the same key messages. The pre-tour campaign communicated with the target audience via editorial content and competitions and the on-tour campaign used photo opportunities of the players in environments away from the rugby field thus achieving greater brand standout for NTL and again driving the message of NTL having exclusive behind-the-scenes access to the players. A key requirement of the PR campaign was to inform the target audience about NTL's products and services. This was done using the theme 'Technology on Tour' whereby NTL brought tangible benefits to the players in return for PR, e.g. videoconferencing facilities. PR was also driven regionally through player appearances in key areas for local press promotions.

Sponsorship leverage activities targeting customers concentrated on three areas – third parties, concessions and acquisitions. Lions-themed customer communications across all mediums were used, from direct mailers to almost 1 million homes, to door drops, regional radio ads and bill stuffers.

The sponsorship was driven internally by different divisions within the business who each undertook their own promotional activities. The Business and Broadcast Divisions sent a direct mailer to 5,865 prospective clients and invitations to 350 top customers to go on tour to Australia. NTL's interactive division used the sponsorship to increase the use of NTL interactive TV by using exclusive Lions Tour content and providing coverage of the Tour in the form of news, statistics, results, player profiles, a fantasy game and transcripts of video diaries of the players. NTL's content division, PTV, produced a quality video using behind-the-scenes footage exclusive to NTL. This was sold after the Tour and positioned PTV as a major player in sports television production. The revenue from sales of the video resulted in the filming being self-liquidating. The Lions Tour video provided a perfect illustration of the way in which many of NTL's division's came together through the sponsorship with PTV shooting the footage, Business and Consumer divisions using the video as a door opener to prospective customers, Interactive and New Media using it for content on the NTL.com/lions website and Internal Communications using it to send daily transcripts of the Diary of a Lion to all staff via the intranet.

Internal Communications also used other elements of the sponsorship to build internal pride and morale. Staff received information relating to the Tour before it was made public. Lions-themed competitions were set up with prizes ranging from trips to meet the players to a six-week supply of chocolates. A giant tour shirt was also taken on a tour of NTL offices and staff were invited to write messages of good luck to the team on the shirt which was later presented to the players by NTL employees.

NTL's leverage of the sponsorship resulted in 33 per cent of the target audience being aware of the sponsorship post the Tour. This rose to 62 per cent amongst those who had watched more than five hours of the television coverage. In comparison, Vodafone's association with the English cricket team during the Ashes Series, which took place at the same time, generated spontaneous awareness of 25 per cent for Vodafone as the team sponsor and this was the third year of Vodafone's sponsorship.

More importantly in terms of NTL's objectives, post-tour research indicated that 83 per cent of respondents described NTL as a telephone, TV and internet company, with 57 per cent of respondents associating NTL with broadband thus demonstrating the effectiveness of the sponsorship in informing customers about what the company actually did.

The NTL.com/lions website proved to be a huge success with the site enjoying over 850,000 hits during one week of the Tour, and 250,000 page impressions and 77,000 unique users over the six week duration of the Tour. To put this into perspective, TV's reality show, *Big Brother* in the UK, had 85,000 unique users over eight weeks during the same period. Specific elements of the site had the following results – 'Diary of a Lion' had 27,000 streams per day and over 100,000 people played the fantasy Lions game.

The PR campaign generated over £2 million worth of brand exposure in the six weeks of the Lions Tour of which over £350,000 was generated by PR activity through editorial lifestyle pieces and competitions.

KEY INSIGHT

The success of NTL's sponsorship of the Lions team in 2001 is largely attributable to the way in which the sponsorship was embraced by all divisions within the NTL network. NTL's exposure through shirt branding and signage was only the tip of the iceberg and it was the co-ordinated exploitation of the sponsorship by all divisions of NTL that ensured its overwhelming effectiveness in raising awareness of NTL's products as well as in achieving NTL's internal objectives of building staff morale and uniting NTL's diverse business divisions.

Individual Endorsement

Individuals present some interesting opportunities for sponsors, particularly 'off the field' of play where product endorsements are commonplace amongst the top performing and recognized athletes. Such opportunities exist around both individual athletes and athletes that compete in teams.

So for example, Michael Johnson, while playing for the Chicago Bulls in the NBA was not entitled to carry any sponsor branding on his playing strip while competing but enjoyed a string of endorsements while off the court.

In certain individual sports, e.g., tennis or golf, opportunities may exist for logo placement on the athlete's clothing.

Individual sponsorship and/or endorsement rights are normally managed by sponsorship agencies on behalf of the athletes themselves and are separate to any rights associated with the events that the athletes may participate in.

One of the most successful athlete endorsement campaigns of late is that managed by Octagon for Anna Kournikova who, alongside the likes of the

Williams sisters and Martina Hingis, has attracted the attention of the sports fans worldwide both on and off the court.

CASE STUDY

Anna Kournikova: the power of athlete endorsements

Anna Kournikova is the most sought after and photographed female athlete in the world. She exudes glamour and her stunning good looks, coupled with her talent on the tennis court, make her a marketer's dream even though she has yet to win a WTA tour title. She is an athlete that transcends her sport and her appeal goes far beyond the world of tennis. She is a symbol that reaches an audience that goes beyond age groups, gender and interests.

Companies have been keen to capitalize on Anna's global influence and selling power by entering into endorsement agreements with her. Two of her major sponsors are Adidas and Lycos both of whom can show tangible benefits from their association with Anna and regard her as an integral part of their marketing efforts.

Figure 5.1 Anna Kournikova in Adidas suit. Reprinted with permission from Getty Images. Clive Brunskill, photographer

Figure 5.2 Anna Kournikova in Adidas tennis dress. Reprinted with permission from Getty Images. Clive Brunskill, photographer

Adidas

Adidas has always been associated with the top players and personalities in the world of tennis. Anna Kournikova continues this pattern, following in the footsteps of previous tennis greats such as Rod Laver, Ille Nastase, Steffi Graf and Stefan Edberg. The partnership makes further sense in that Adidas and Anna both convey brand values of inspiration, inventiveness and commitment.

Anna is one of the few athletes today who sets trends in the design and fashion world. Her on-court apparel, footwear and image have an influence that extends well beyond tennis thus making her even more of an asset to Adidas. Her style is an influencing factor in both the world of performance tennis apparel and footwear and casual street wear.

Anna has been used by Adidas in five global television advertising campaigns. Some campaigns, such as the 'Made in Russia' campaign (1998), feature Anna only whereas others use a selection of Adidas sponsored athletes e.g. the 'Welcome to the Tennis Club' campaign (2000) which featured Martina Hingis, Marat Safin and Jan-Michael Gambill along with Anna or the 2002 ClimaCool campaign which featured Anna together with David Beckham and Ian Thorpe. It is worth noting that Anna is the only Adidas athlete to have been featured in as many advertising campaigns in the past five years which demonstrates her importance to Adidas and her influence in the marketplace.

Anna's impact on the Adidas brand is far-reaching. She has played a significant role not only in strengthening the brand's reputation as a leader in tennis, but Anna's ability to transcend her sport, coupled with the trendsetting apparel that Adidas and Anna have introduced, has given the brand credibility as an innovative, leading casual streetwear brand as well. Anna's selling power is well illustrated by the fact that when she debuts a new outfit prior to each of the Grand Slams, these high-dollar, limited-edition outfits are immediately sold out of shops around the world.

Lycos

Lycos is a leading internet portal, offering users a fast, easy and efficient mechanism to make effective use of the internet and manage its vast resources. The company's vision is to become the most visited online destination in the world by providing users with a compelling network of web brands, internet services and next-generation communication technologies.

Lycos identified that Anna Kournikova was the most searched for athlete in the world on the internet, generating more searches than Tiger Woods, Mia Hamm and Michael Jordan combined. Few people, even outside of sport, can claim to have such 'pulling power'. In recognition of this, Lycos created an award which was handed to Anna at Wimbledon in June 2000. This resulted in global PR exposure for both Anna and for Lycos and demonstrated her power as a global icon.

Following on from this success, and because of the brand synergies that existed in that both Lycos and Anna encapsulate the brand personality of being fun, sexy, irreverent and global, Lycos decided to further capitalize on Anna's influence by entering into a multi-year agreement with her. Using its association with Anna, Lycos initiated an online promotion to generate awareness around its different offerings, from sport to finance, by tapping into the different passions of consumers and offering them the opportunity of winning free Anna Kournikova products and merchandise ranging from Adidas clothing, Yonex tennis equipment and Omega watches to motor vehicles.

Lycos also set up Anna Kournikova's personal website which has accumulated a database of close to 300,000 people. The website offers fans the opportunity to download pictures of Anna, to view many of her sponsor's advertising campaigns, to chat online to other fans, to send mail to Anna and to keep abreast of Anna's latest results on the WTA Tour.

The Anna Kournikova marketing endorsement has been integrated online and offline in many facets. Besides the online promotion Lycos has used Kournikova in a number of advertising campaigns – a billboard advertising campaign in popular cities including Times Square, New York, in a print ad campaign in *Sports Illustrated* and in two television commercials which appeared on network and cable television in the United States. Lycos has also maximized PR opportunities by holding press conferences at key Grand Slam events such as Wimbledon and the US Open.

Figure 5.3 Anna Kournikova relaxes by the pool in Adidas apparel. Reprinted with permission from Getty Images. Clive Brunskill, photographer

Ben Sturner, Sports Marketing Manager for the Lycos Network sums up the success of Lycos' association with Anna – 'Our marketing campaign with Anna Kournikova has been the most successful online/offline promotion in the history of the Lycos Network. The television commercials were highly effective, as we tracked studies which show that males 18–34 years are now more likely to use Lycos after viewing the spots. Her official site on Lycos has attracted more than 300,000 members from more than 200 countries around the world ranging from as far away as Columbia to Cameroon. Anna's global appeal clearly transcends the sport of tennis and is the perfect fit with the Lycos brand.'

KEY INSIGHT

Anna Kournikova is an athlete with substantial celebrity leverage. She's a young, brilliant, professional athlete whose celebrity extends well beyond the world of tennis and the tennis court – she has captured the public's imagination in mainstream newspapers, magazines and tabloids – and represents a powerful and influential marketing platform for brands associated with her.

Not just individual athletes

Security company Maxidor took advantage of a tactical opportunity to sponsor something quite out of the ordinary – Max the Gorilla. This is a great example of how passion branding can be applied to even the most unlikely platform.

CASE STUDY

Maxidor's sponsorship of Max the Gorilla and the Johannesburg Zoo: Identifying small tactical sponsorship opportunities that deliver big results

Maxidor is one of South Africa's leading manufacturers of physical security barriers. It is a well-established company with over 15 years experience in the security industry offering a wide range of patented, custom-made products to satisfy domestic and commercial security requirements.

Maxidor was the first in many product developments which today are considered standards in the security industry, for example, 'Slamlock' to name but one. Furthermore, Maxidor always placed a great investment in educating the public in the importance of physical security barriers as well as proper security routines and disciplines. Maxidor were renowned as the 'security experts' but were not 'top of mind' and the company therefore needed to find an effective way in which to drive 'top of mind' brand awareness and overcome the disadvantage it faced in that the generic name of some competing products placed some competitors more easily in the minds of potential customers.

The Johannesburg Zoo and one of its most loved animals, Max the Gorilla, provided the perfect sponsorship opportunity for Maxidor. The Zoo enjoyed strong support from the local community and people of all ages showed a strong emotional attachment to Max the Gorilla, a gentle giant who generated a considerable amount of media coverage. An association with the Zoo and Max portrayed Maxidor as a company actively committed to the community and had the potential to deliver a far-reaching, positive connection with Maxidor's target audience, namely affluent, community-oriented family people for whom safety was a concern. In addition, the name link with Max would help to raise top of mind awareness of the Maxidor name. There was a further bonus in that Max the Gorilla had been bestowed with the 'Crime Fighter of the Year' award because of his heroic survival from a shotgun attack made by a runaway burglar and this created a direct connection with Maxidor's line of business.

A media function was held announcing Maxidor's adoption of Max the Gorilla and its association with the Zoo in the form of a cash donation and the supply of security products throughout the Zoo's offices and education centre. In return Maxidor received branding in prominent places within the Zoo.

Maxidor ran a print advertising campaign highlighting its link with Max. This was carried in the major national weekend newspaper to coincide with the adoption announcement and then in leading home and lifestyle magazines for three months thereafter. Live reads were also carried on radio during the week the adoption was announced to generate further publicity.

Maxidor's staff embraced the sponsorship and participated in a Johannesburg Zoo corporate fundraiser event – 'Spinning with Max'. Maxidor received prominent branding at this event – its participating team wore branded kit, Maxidor boards were placed at the ticket office, on the path to and inside Max's enclosure and a Maxidor corporate stand was placed at Max's enclosure for those visiting the Zoo to view the company's product range. All Maxidor staff were invited to spend the day at the Zoo and were treated to a special two-hour guided tour.

Maxidor also communicated the sponsorship through its corporate brochure, printing an additional 250,000 brochures containing pictures of the media function which announced the sponsorship and these were distributed nationally. In addition, Maxidor used its switchboard answering system to convey valuable messages to the public about the Johannesburg Zoo and how they could go about making donations or adopting an animal. Self-addressed postage-paid envelopes were printed to promote donations to the Zoo. These envelopes were handed out by Maxidor consultants nationwide to each client they met. Contributions made by the public went directly to the Johannesburg Zoo. To further highlight the name link with Max the Gorilla, Maxidor modified its corporate logo by changing the colour of the letters MAX to distinguish them from the rest of the Maxidor company name and draw attention to their association with Max the Gorilla.

The success of the sponsorship was evidenced by the increase in good quality leads. Customers bought from Maxidor because of its association with the Zoo and Max the Gorilla. The public perception of the company improved almost immediately and Maxidor was regarded as being a caring company. The company benefited further in that there was an increased request for franchising opportunities and internally, staff morale was boosted which positively impacted on the work environment. Maxidor experienced an average growth of 85 per cent growth per annum, purchased its own assembly plant in Johannesburg, Cape Town and Durban, doubled its export portfolio and became one of the top 300 companies in South Africa 2002/2003, much of which was due to a simple marketing act that changed the future of the company.

KEY INSIGHT

This sponsorship demonstrates that great results can be achieved even in the case of small-scale sponsorships provided there is a sound strategic link between the brand and the passion branding platform and if the leverage activities are well thought through and co-ordinated to deliver a focused and consistent message.

Leading Thought
David Butler, *Head of Laureus Sport For Good Foundation and Manager of Laureus World Sports Academy*

There are three very positive universal languages; love, music and sport – all of which are tremendously powerful tools if incorporated effectively in a growingly cynical – and global – consumer market. Gauging that cynicism is essential to any campaign – there can be few more heinous marketing crimes than mis-exploitation of a holy grail.

Fan passion is a powerful vehicle. For instance, take Daley Thompson as a role model in the 1980s for Lucozade and decathlon video games – overnight he changed a brand and created a phenomenon. He was one of the first athletes to be used in such a context and a powerful example of how fan passion can be accessed to change perceptions and create new environments.

Michael Jordan's superhuman feats and marketability helped create and focus one of the world's leading sports brands as well as carry a major influence – if not essential influence – over the success of the NBA.

Other key brands, more noticeably Coca-Cola, are actively moving into the realm of fan association rather than player association. Be a fan, live the whole experience through the product. Brilliant. This is a major trend in sponsorship that is now leading to a further development – social marketing. Consumers are not dummies and are becoming increasingly sophisticated – and exhausted.

It is no longer enough to wear the product and be like the athlete; consumers and fans are wanting to know what is *behind* the product.

Advertising and marketing give the consumer an image that the ego buys into. More and more however, consumers are wanting a product that matches their beliefs; whether it be against animal-testing or the exploitation of children.

Brands can tie into fan passion – and athletes can play a role in championing this link – if the product is up to it.

Stadium sponsorship

Stadium sponsorships provide sponsors with the opportunity to associate themselves with a stadium, primarily by way of naming rights, e.g. 3Com Park (formerly Candlestick Park, home of the San Francisco 49ers American Football team). In addition, the sponsor would typically secure a range of additional rights – from hospitality rights, e.g. suite/s at the venue and tickets to events staged at the venue, venue signage, vending rights and the like.

The major benefit of such a sponsorship is one of awareness with all promotion relating to events being staged at the venue referring to the stadium by name. In addition, a number of business benefits can be built into these sponsorships such as vending rights which, depending on the product category, can be very meaningful.

Sponsorship deals concluded in this area tend to be long-term by nature, i.e. ten years plus in duration.

It does however pay to consider such sponsorships with a degree of caution, particularly where the community may have strong emotional links to the stadium and may react negatively to a name change as was the case in Cape Town with Newlands Stadium, considered by most to be the home of rugby in South Africa.

Few would have anticipated the backlash against new stadium sponsors Norwich who, in return for a significant cash sponsorship, had opted to change the name of the stadium to Norwich Park Newlands. When making the announcement the Norwich CEO was booed by fans, disgruntled with the financial services company for its tampering with tradition.

Broadcast sponsorship

Broadcast sponsorship involves the 'labelling' of a television broadcast by a sponsor who may, or may not also be the event sponsor.

The extent to which a sponsor may brand a broadcast differs from market to market and depends on the broadcast regulations in those markets.

In South Africa, for example, a typical broadcast sponsorship on the national broadcaster the SABC around a 30-minute programme would include a 10–15 second opening and closing billboard, on-screen corner sponsor's logo for up to 50 per cent of the duration of the broadcast, 5 second stings leading to and from commercial ad breaks and two 5 second squeeze-backs. In addition, an allocation of 30-second programme promo spots would be included and, depending on the value of the sponsorship, an allocation of classical advertising spots.

By contrast, the BBC in the UK does not allow any commercial branding around their programmes which limits sponsors of events broadcast on the channel to incidental exposure that they may be able to generate through event signage.

Broadcast sponsorships can apply to all genres of television programming from sport to music to entertainment.

Another form of broadcast sponsorship, far less subtle but no less effective, is that of product placement where a sponsor's products are 'dropped' into the programme script. It is no coincidence that James Bond now drives the latest BMW or that Pop Stars contestants have access to Coca-Cola on demand.

Typically, broadcasters will afford event sponsors the first right of refusal to take up a broadcast sponsorship around the broadcast of their event. If declined however, the broadcaster will typically have the right to offer the broadcast sponsorship to any sponsor.

Another type of broadcast sponsorships that is gaining popularity around the world is that of advertiser-funded programming. In such instances, a sponsor will pay for the production costs of a television programme which will then be offered to a broadcaster on a 'barter' basis, i.e. broadcast rights to the programme in return not for cash but rather a package of on-air promotional elements similar to those highlighted above.

This type of broadcast sponsorship is sometimes referred to as brand casting due to the fact that the sponsor has the ability, to some extent, to influence the production values of the programme being sponsored and in the process to ensure that their brand identity and key messages are woven into the fabric of the programme as opposed to just using the programme as a badging opportunity.

A long-standing example of such an arrangement is *Gillette World Sport Special* which is produced centrally in London by Sunset & Vine with production costs paid for by Gillette and distributed worldwide for broadcast in hundreds of countries. As part of the deal, Gillette secures exposure around the world at a fraction of the cost of what it would cost to buy the same commercial airtime. The world's broadcasters get a top-class sports programme without any direct financial outlay while being able to generate revenue for themselves through the sale of advertising during the programme.

Another great example is Western Union World of Soccer produced by Octagon CSI in London and now distributed to over 206 broadcasters around the world.

Leading Thought
Karl Bistany, *Managing Director for Europe, Africa and Australasia and President of Television for Octagon Worldwide*

Western Union is essentially a money-transfer company. Their key target market is individual consumers and primarily immigrant workers around the world and their families.

If you look at any migration pattern around the world, there are tens maybe hundreds of millions of migrant workers throughout the globe, making consumer targeting quite a challenge. We spent probably six months with Western Union trying to identify suitable opportunities to reach their consumers. The common denominator we found, albeit that it only covered about 85–90 per cent of the audience we were trying to reach, was soccer.

In response, we came about with the idea of producing a global soccer show which would be given away to broadcasters and in return, the broadcasters would not only carry the fairly prominent Western Union branding in and around the show, but we would also barter ad spots and give them back to Western Union.

For Western Union it made sense for a number of reasons. First of all, they had set themselves a target of growing their business by 50 per cent in 3 years and creating awareness was therefore an important objective for them. Because their consumers are spread out across the world however, an above-the-line advertising campaign would have cost them somewhere around the $60 million mark and their budget was far less than that. What we offered them was essentially a global weekly advertising campaign that is very cost effective to the extent that currently we're in about 206 countries with most broadcasters showing each week's show three to four times.

Western Union then started to leverage the show locally and began to receive a lot of 'invisible' benefits through local competitions, local TV shows, local radio shows and so on that tied in with the TV show and that's where they got what I call, the 'icing on the cake'.

So for Western Union, the show provided an ideal way of essentially having a global weekly advertising campaign using soccer as the platform which is clearly what most of their consumers are interested in. A lot of the editorial content in the show is not focused on top-level playing football but rather on local interest stories such as for example a story from Calcutta or a story from Lagos which potential and current Western Union consumers can relate to. It's about soccer and it does feature some of their favourite stars but it also talks about the guys in their street who play and aspire to play in the African Nations Cup for example.

In evaluating their return on investment, there are two points of valuation. The first is the rate card value of the bartered ad spots which are utilized by Western Union as standard above-the-line advertising (TVCs) plus the opening and closing titles and break bumpers. The evaluation comes in at five times media spend. So for every dollar Western Union spend they get five back in media value – and that excludes the value of any local leverage programmes. The combined valuation comes in at around five to seven times media spend. So for every dollar that Western Union spend they get five to seven back in media value – and that excludes the value of any local leverage programmes.

The second valuation relates to the 'in-vision' branding received by way of graphic straps. Whilst more difficult to provide a finite value this inventory is arguably more valuable as it is deemed 'in-programming' branding and thus does not suffer from the traditional problems of viewer advertiser avoidance. For example, whenever a graphic comes up during the show, such as when interviewing say David Beckham, the Western Union logo comes up with a rotating globe so you can't miss it. Western Union accept that this has value but don't wish to include it in the valuation process. By our calculation that would increase that multiple to seven.

Broadcasters are happy to participate in this type of arrangement, first and foremost because it is actually good programming – soccer is a common denominator so they can get ratings around it. Secondly, there is no cost to them apart from giving up the ad spots. So in that sense, and particularly at a time when broadcasters are looking to make a saving, it is a win-win situation – it is trying to understand the broadcaster's perspective but also understanding the sponsor's needs – having a meeting of minds.

Multi-sponsor events

As the costs of staging major events has rapidly grown, organizers and promoters have been forced to look at creative ways to package their rights. The most common approach in such instances is to divide the available rights amongst a stable of non-competing sponsors as is done very successfully for events like the Olympic Games and World Cup Soccer.

From a sponsor's perspective, the most important feature of such multi-sponsor programmes is that of category exclusivity – the theory being that as long as no competitor has access to the rights then they are as good as sole rights. This is true but only up to a point as too many sponsors can create a cluttered environment where it can be become difficult to be noticed.

The success or failure of such programmes really comes down to the professionalism of the organizers or promoters and their ability to effectively balance their need for funds and the value of the rights offered to sponsors. Added to this is the greater importance of leveraging by the sponsor to ensure that their association with the event is noticed by the fans.

Cause related marketing

Definition of cause related marketing

The most appropriate definition of cause related marketing that I have come across is provided by Hamish Pringle and Marjorie Thompson in their wonderful book *Brand Spirit*.[1]

> *Cause Related Marketing can be defined as a strategic positioning and marketing tool which links a company or brand to a relevant social cause or issue for mutual benefit.*

---

[1] Hamish Pringle & Marjorie Thompson, *Brand Spirit: how cause related marketing builds brands* (London; John Wiley & Sons: 1999). This is undoubtedly the best book that I have come across on the subject of cause related marketing and is well worth spending some quality time with. The thoughts and ideas that the authors cover are equally applicable to the other types of passion platforms covered in *Passion Branding*.

Cause related marketing is much like sport and entertainment marketing in that it aligns a company or brand with a group of consumers that are passionate about a particular subject. The only real difference between the two is that the nature of the platform provided by cause related marketing tends to be charitable or cause related rather than sports or entertainment oriented.

Another feature of cause related marketing that differentiates it from traditional sports and entertainment marketing to some extent is the fact that the relationship between a company or brand and charity or cause tends to be more symbiotic in nature. Cause related marketing also provides companies and brands with the potential to directly address a social cause or issue to a much greater extent than would normally be possible in the world of sports which tends to be regulated to a far greater degree.

This is not about donations or handouts. It is about doing good and taking full advantage of that fact for the benefit of your brand and your business. It is something that you talk about doing and which you should integrate into the fabric of your business with a view to positively influencing the way that consumers, staff and suppliers feel about your brand and about doing business with you.

In the process, the charity or social cause receives a business partner that can provide much sought after funding as well as enhanced awareness for its brand and cause.

Leading Thought
Michael Brockbank, *Vice President Brand Communication, Unilever*

We have had very successful experiences with cause-related sponsorship. Bushell's is our leading Australian tea-brand. It offers consumers the benefits of revival and refreshment. It's seen as a typical down to earth Aussie brand.

Match that to a typical, down-to-earth Aussie problem. With its huge landmass and tiny population, Australia has a real road-safety issue, caused by driver fatigue, especially as the unwary try to drive long distances over holiday weekends. Community groups try to address this problem by encouraging drivers to refresh and revive themselves at roadside rest stops. A perfect opportunity for Bushell's.

Here is a great fit of values, a clear appeal to the passion of the consumer for road safety and an extremely well leveraged campaign (to the extent that it was featured in government-funded communication).

500,000 motorists were sampled with a free cup of Bushell's last year – that's 3 per cent of all Australian drivers. The image profile of the brand has improved, and 12 per cent of the total budget now goes to the sponsorship.

Cause Related Marketing and brand identity

A number of companies have started using cause related marketing as an effective communication platform, in some cases as the central theme around which their entire business models are based.

One of the best-known examples is that of The Body Shop which embraced the preservation of the environment and anti-animal testing as the central positioning for the brand. These values were built into every aspect of the Body Shop's business, including all aspects relating to its products, and in so doing The Body Shop was able to claim a territory comprising like-minded ethical consumers while at the same time making a real contribution to the causes it had elected to support. In leveraging this ethical positioning through PR and other low-cost interventions, The Body Shop achieved what many other brands have failed to do with huge advertising budgets – become part of popular culture and establish itself as a recognized international brand.

Cause Related Marketing as a fundraising platform

In addition to making a statement about a company or brand and driving awareness for a charitable or social cause, cause related marketing campaigns often include an element of fundraising whereby consumers are empowered to make a contribution towards a cause and in the process feel good about themselves.

A wonderful example of this was LSE-listed and FTSE 100 financial services group Old Mutual's Save Chapman's Peak Fund which not only proved to be an effective fundraising campaign but also added an additional dimension to Old Mutual's traditional sponsorship of road running.

CASE STUDY

Old Mutual Save Chapman's Peak Fund: linking a cause-related campaign to an existing sponsorship

Old Mutual is one of the leading financial services institutions in South Africa, offering life assurance, asset management, banking and general insurance to over four million South African clients. The nature of Old Mutual's products and services mean that the health, vitality and productivity of the people it serves impact directly on its business. In light of this, Old Mutual values sport as a means to a healthy lifestyle and has always been involved in the sponsorship of sport, particularly road running with its wide appeal and easy accessibility to people from all walks of life. Old Mutual's advertising pay-off line, 'With you every step of the way' also lends itself to road running themed creative executions.

The Old Mutual Two Oceans Marathon is the organization's flagship road running sponsorship and one of the most popular events on the road running calendar attracting over 15,000 runners each year, a growing proportion of whom are overseas participants.

The main race is an ultra marathon run along possibly one of the most scenic pieces of coastline in the world. However, in 2000, due to a runaway fire and massive rock slides, the most dramatic section of the route, Chapman's Peak Drive along the Atlantic Ocean coastline, had to be closed to the public in order for much needed, long-term repair work to be carried out and the organisers were therefore forced to alter the ultra marathon route. This caused widespread comment from participants because this section of the route in particular formed such an integral part of their enjoyment of the race and they therefore wanted to ensure that it could be reinstated in future.

In response, and with a view to making a valuable contribution towards addressing the environmental challenges facing one of South Africa's most spectacular tourist attractions, Old Mutual founded the Save Chapman's Peak Fund as a cause related marketing extension of its sponsorship of the Two Oceans Marathon.

Old Mutual made an initial cash injection of R100,000 and then set about implementing a number of initiatives aimed at garnering support for the Fund by calling on the support of the local community and participating runners. A key component of the campaign was an initiative whereby all race participants received a pair of high quality green running socks and were encouraged to wear them on race day to demonstrate their support of the Save Chapman's Peak Fund. Old Mutual pledged a R5 donation to the fund for every athlete who finished the race wearing the official green socks. More than half the field took part in the campaign which resulted in almost R30,000 being raised for the fund from this initiative alone and post-event research indicated that 90 per cent of the runners thought that the green sock campaign was worthwhile.

In order to generate awareness of the Fund amongst the general public, the Save Chapman's Peak Fund was included in all race press releases and PR activity and a website was created which was also linked to both the official race website and the Old Mutual corporate website. In addition, Old Mutual used its weekly endurance sports television show to flight promotional inserts explaining the Save Chapman's Peak Fund and how one could go about pledging a donation to the fund by phoning the specially designated pledge line. On race day, the pledge line was operational during the entire five-hour

Figure 5.4 Chapman's Peak Damage. Reprinted with permission from Old Mutual plc (photograph supplied by Shawn Benjamin, www.arkimages.com)

Figure 5.5 Chapman's Peak Damage. Reprinted with permission from Old Mutual plc (photograph supplied by Shawn Benjamin, www.arkimages.com)

live broadcast and was punted regularly by the commentators. As a result of these activities, post-event research showed that 63 per cent of participants were aware of the link between Old Mutual's green sock campaign and the Save Chapman's Peak Fund.

In order to maintain momentum after race day, Old Mutual planned other initiatives during the year which were aimed at raising further funds for the repair of Chapman's Peak. The Cape Philharmonic Orchestra held an open-air concert at the foot of Chapman's Peak and invited people to

Figure 5.6 The Green Sock campaign. Reprinted with permission from Old Mutual plc

come and enjoy the music while picnicking. The money raised from ticket sales was put towards the Fund. Chapman's Peak water was also bottled and sold which raised further funds.

In total almost three quarters of a million rand was raised for the Save Chapman's Peak Fund in less than a year. The road is however still closed but, thanks to the efforts of Old Mutual, the local community and the participants in the Old Mutual Two Oceans Marathon, the local municipality has been able to begin the necessary repair work which should see this landmark being re-opened in the next year or so.

KEY INSIGHT

Global trends show that consumers want companies to support causes that are personally relevant to them and if a company is to benefit from associating with a cause, the link must be logical in the minds of the consumer. Old Mutual's link with the Save Chapman's Peak Fund fulfilled both of these criteria and elicited a

Figure 5.7 Old Mutual Two Oceans Marathon Runners Along Chapman's Peak Drive. Reprinted with permission from Old Mutual plc (photograph supplied by Shawn Benjamin, www.arkimages.com)

highly emotional response from the local community and race participants because the closure of Chapman's Peak directly affected them all. For this reason, Old Mutual was able to gain support for its efforts and make a worthwhile contribution towards the repair of Chapman's Peak.

Social Responsibility Marketing

Historically the responsibility of Corporate Social Investment departments and Corporate Foundations were focussed around donations for worthy causes; now, social responsibility marketing is coming of age as an effective stand-alone marketing platform. Corporates have historically been shy to claim any benefit from their altruistic efforts believing that being socially responsible was something that one did rather than spoke about having done. This is however changing as companies and brands are increasingly starting to feel comfortable talking about their investments into communities and consumers see no wrong in them doing so.

Definition of Social Responsibility Marketing

Social Responsibility Marketing involves the combination of do-good corporate initiatives with objective-driven marketing and communications campaigns.

South African Experience

South Africa's transition from apartheid to democracy has many lessons from which the developed world can learn in the area of social responsibility marketing.

South Africa has been plagued with a history of separate development. As a result, a huge portion of its population have not previously had access to, amongst other things, opportunities to participate in sport. Development programmes have therefore become a major component of most South African sports sponsorship programmes.

In so doing, South African sponsors have been combining their high-profile 'élite' sponsorships such as the title sponsorship of an international event like the Engen Grand Prix Summer Series Athletics with a low profile 'social' component as, for example, talent identification systems like the Engen Talent Search, and in the process demonstrating their brand's commitment to the New South Africa and its people.

Laureus Sport For Good Foundation

The power of sport to bring about meaningful change has recently been recognized by two global brands, Richemont and DaimlerChrysler. As groups comprising a number of global luxury brands, the two jointly established the Laureus concept as a way of bringing about social change in the world through the platform of sport.

Laureus, although established only a few years ago, has quickly captured the imagination of athletes, sports fans and broadcasters worldwide. The Laureus Sports Academy enjoys a membership of 42 of the world's leading athletes, the Laureus Sports Awards has become recognized as the Oscars of sport and was watched by over 5 billion people in 2002 and the Laureus Sport For Good Foundation financially supports over 13 social initiatives around the world.

The marketing benefits realized by these two groups as a result of their forward thinking initiative have been significant and demonstrate the potential that brands and corporates have to bring about meaningful change whilst still making a profit.

CASE STUDY

Laureus Sport For Good: recognizing the power of sport as a mechanism to bring about social change

In today's society it is consumer brands and their corporate custodians that have the power to bring about social change rather than the politicians that society traditionally turned to. Recognizing this, the Laureus Sport for Good Foundation was established in 1999 by founding patrons DaimlerChrysler and Richemont with the aim of providing opportunities for positive social progress across the world using the power of sport.

Laureus is the Latin word for 'laurel', the universal symbol for victory in sport, and the Laureus brand encapsulates the following values – aspirant, global/universal, multi-dimensional (sport, lifestyle, philanthropy), credibility, compassionate/socially responsible – and represents the best in sport, all of which make Laureus a powerful symbol for social change.

The Laureus brand comprises three integrated components which combine to form a truly unique property. These components are the Laureus World Sports Awards, the Laureus World Sports Academy and the Laureus Sport for Good Foundation.

1. Laureus World Sports Awards

This is a global sports awards programme that honours the world's best sportsmen and women on an annual basis for their achievements across all sporting disciplines and represents the pinnacle of the Laureus year. The awards consist of seven categories, namely:

1. World Sportsman of the Year
2. World Sportswoman of the Year

3. World Team of the Year
4. World Newcomer of the Year
5. World Comeback of the Year
6. World Alternative Sportsperson of the Year
7. World Sportsperson of the Year with a Disability

Five nominees per award are selected by sports editors and journalists from 75 countries who make up the selection panel. All nominations are collated and the top five are put before the Laureus World Sports Academy who elects the winners. A glittering ceremony is held in Monaco to award the winners with a Laureus Statuette and the event is broadcast to more than one billion people in over 170 countries worldwide. Past winners have included Michael Schumacher, Tiger Woods, Jennifer Capriati, Marion Jones, Cathy Freeman and Lance Armstrong to name a few.

The high esteem in which the awards are held is evident in the comments made by some past winners.

- 'This is quite an honour to have this award! It's kind of overwhelming to have my peers around the world choose me as the recipient of this award...I'm humbled and honoured.' – *Tiger Woods, Laureus Sportsman of the Year, 2000*
- 'I'm really honoured to be receiving this award, especially being here tonight with all these tremendous athletes. I didn't realize the magnitude of this award...Laureus is a great organization.' – *Jennifer Capriati, Laureus Comeback of the Year Award Winner, 2001*
- 'What an honour! Thank you everybody...thank you Laureus! Just to be on the same stage as all those who came before me...Just to be considered and mentioned among some of the greatest [athletes].' – *Marion Jones, Laureus Sportswoman of the Year Award Winner, 2000.*

2. Laureus World Sports Academy

The Academy consists of 43 of the world's most legendary athletes who have each made an outstanding contribution to world sport. Members are responsible for selecting the Laureus World Sports' Award winners and act as guardians and goodwill ambassadors for the Laureus Sport for Good Foundation. Members give of their time voluntarily to support the Foundation's projects and enhance the influence of sport in the wider society because of their belief in their power as sporting icons to raise awareness and make a difference with respect to a number of worthy social causes around the world.

Members include sporting legends such as Michael Jordan, Sebastian Coe, Mark Spitz, Daley Thompson, Kapil Dev, Boris Becker, Edwin Moses, Jack Nicklaus, Nadia Comaneci, Sean Fitzpatrick, Katarina Witt and Pele to name a few.

While the Laureus World Sports Awards celebrate the very best in sporting achievements at its annual event, the Academy, through its work on the ground, aims to celebrate the very best in human achievement every day.

3. Laureus Sport for Good Foundation

This is the *raison d'être* or soul of the Laureus brand and is an innovative charitable initiative which uses the positive influence of sport to tackle society's most pressing social challenges around the globe.

Sport has a unique power to unite people behind a common desire and evoke a strongly emotional response from people. It provides a point of commonality for people from different walks of life and it is because of powerful characteristics such as these that sport can be harnessed to bring about social change whether it be crime, drug abuse, community regeneration, peace or cross-border initiatives.

The Foundation is committed to year round activities and fundraising initiatives which are used currently to benefit 12 charitable programmes on five continents. These programmes are as follows:

1. Sport for Good New York   New York, USA
2. Midnight Basketball League   Richmond, Virginia, USA
3. KICK   Berlin, Germany
4. Youth Sport Foyle   Ireland

 5. Mathare Youth Sports Association   Nairobi, Kenya
 6. Unified Sports Programme,   Czech Republic, Slovakia
    Special Olympics   and China
 7. Street Universe   Cape Town, South Africa
 8. Nakulabye Community Aids Project   Uganda
 9. Indigenous Sports Program   Australia
10. Futbol Futur   Argentina
11. Training for Peace   Middle East
12. Women in Sport   Morocco

Founder patrons, DaimlerChrysler and Richemont, each donate US$1 million a year to the Laureus Sport for Good Foundation to be used to fund the programmes it supports. The maximum a project can receive in one year is US$100,000 and the Foundation closely monitors each project to ensure that the funds are utilized in the most effective manner. The Foundation supports a project for a minimum of three years.

The Global Reach of Laureus

The powerful effect of the coming together of sports and social responsibility marketing to create a hugely relevant platform is evident when one considers the global reach and tangible positive changes that Laureus has managed to bring about in its three years of existence.

- The Laureus Sports Awards is broadcast as a two-hour television programme to an audience of 1.6 billion people in 172 countries.
- Laureus occupies more than US$100 million in television airtime on principally terrestrial broadcasters.
- The 2001 Sports Awards event accommodated 1,200 accredited media in addition to the 80 press releases which were distributed to a global network of 6,000 journalists. Over 2,260 articles worth US$40 million in PR value was generated with coverage over a broad spectrum – sport, entertainment, consumer and glamour. Two thousand one hundred photographic images were distributed through the Getty News Global Network/All Sport and the website (www.laureus.com) had 1.5 million hits.

- The Laureus Sport For Good Foundation is making an impact 365 days of the year through its 12 charitable projects that are promoted by 43 of the world's greatest sporting legends.

Across all sports and disciplines, Laureus is not sport or region specific but rather possesses universal appeal in all major markets. It is represented by the most trusted and influential messengers in the world – sporting icons – who are revered the world over and who have a unique power to initiate social change through their endeavours.

KEY INSIGHT

Laureus demonstrates the effectiveness of combining sport and social responsibility marketing to create a powerful medium that started as a small idea but grew under its own energy and enthusiasm so that today it supports programmes around the world 365 days of the year.

Leading Thought
Sean O'Neill, *Brand and Market Communication Director, Diageo*

Corporate social responsibility is one of the most important areas within our business and is one of the greatest challenges facing any organization doing business today. Sponsorship can help meet that challenge, again providing you know your stakeholders and you know what objectives you want to achieve.

Investment without involvement is doomed to fail. As with brand sponsorships, an organization needs to have focus, interest, involvement and investment to truly make a success of projects which fall into the social responsibility arena.

I represent our brands on the board of the Diageo Foundation – the company's charitable arm which helps focus and fund projects which fall into the area of corporate social responsibility. As a trustee, I would never accept or propose an idea from any of the brands that did not have the concept of mutual benefit at its heart. A strong project needs a clear community or social benefit first and foremost. That though needs to be balanced by an appropriate level of brand or organizational benefit, and that's simply because we know that these sort of projects works best when this balance is present. So we're quite open about our approach not being just one of we give money we walk away. It's about mutual benefit with the over-riding factor being there has to be a clear and deliverable social benefit.

Public Private Sector Co-operative Marketing

Public private sector partnerships in the area of sponsorships are becoming more common as the benefits of such an approach to all parties become evident.

A major benefit to a sponsor of being involved in such sponsorships are that, more often than not, they provide the sponsor with the opportunity to leverage their budgets very effectively beyond what would have been possible if they had acted alone. They also provide the sponsor with the opportunity to contribute towards the management of the event or activity and in the process transfer skills between themselves and their public sector counterparts.

Typically in these types of scenarios the public sector will underwrite or provide seed capital for the event or activity and look to the private sector to make up the shortfall in return for a range of benefits that usually extend beyond the traditional rights afforded sponsors. In almost all cases, such events or activities are aimed at some sort of initiative from which the community as a whole, or in part, benefits with tourism, education, job creation, health services or the like being the focus.

Probably the biggest example of this comes from the Olympic movement. Funding for the modern day Olympics comprises a mix of public and private sector support with the latter being contributed predominantly by broadcasters and sponsors. In the process, sponsors are not only deriving a direct benefit for their brands but they are also assisting with the economic development of the host city. The Australian Tourism Commission saw this opportunity and worked the Sydney Olympics to drive significant benefits for Australia's tourism industry. The various sponsors of the Sydney Olympics can confidently claim some of the credit in having helped to make the Games such a success for Australia.

Australia is the first Olympic host nation to take full advantage of the Games to vigorously pursue tourism for the benefit of the whole country. It's something we've never seen take place on this level before, and it's a model that we would like to see carried forward to future Olympic Games in Athens and beyond.
– Michael Payne, Director of Marketing International Olympic Committee.

Government Partnerships

A wonderful example of a successful Government partnership exists in the Proudly South African campaign set up to make a meaningful contribution to job creation in South Africa. The campaign enjoys the support of all stakeholder groups in South Africa including government, the trades union movement, organized business and others, positioning it as a serious initiative with far reaching influence.

Although modelled on similar programmes in the rest of the world, Proudly South African is distinct in one major way and that is in the manner in which it is funded. With insufficient funds available from Government to fund the R150 million initiative in full, the management team at Proudly South African worked with Octagon to develop the PSA Founder Sponsor Programme, a sponsorship programme that would provide sufficient funding to allow the campaign to be run effectively.

The political significance of the campaign, and its ability to provide a powerful platform for companies and brands wanting to position themselves as proudly South African, ensured that the Founder Sponsors programme would be a huge success. Five corporates signed up to the programme very quickly and in the process raised over R60 million for Proudly South Africa.

CASE STUDY

Proudly South African: public private sector co-operative marketing

The idea for the Proudly South African campaign, essentially a job creation mechanism, was devised by organized labour in South Africa. The thinking behind the campaign was that when individuals, and crucially the private and public sectors, engage in purchasing behaviour they will be encouraged to actively think about whether there is a comparable local product when they make consumer choices. This 'free choice' model aims to tap into patriotism to stimulate a greater local share of the market and the added benefits of ensuring quality as well as good labour and environmental practice. The Proudly South African campaign is the first one of its kind in the world that has included fair labour and environmental practice as criteria.

A pre-condition for the success of the campaign was the buy-in from all four constituencies – government, business, labour and community – by the National Economic, Development and Labour Council (Nedlac). Inevitably the conflicting needs and objectives of the various constituencies led to much debate as to the scope and framework of the campaign. In order to facilitate a synergistic approach to the campaign amongst the constituencies and to ensure focus on a common goal, Kaiser Associates were commissioned to conduct market research. Over five intense months, research was conducted into the Nedlac constituencies and consumer attitudes, best practices in similar campaigns run elsewhere, and the desired criteria for membership along with the development of a strategy and a business plan to launch the campaign.

The comprehensive research strongly confirmed the need for a campaign focusing on the origin of the products and services, highlighting criteria they could comply with and showing the benefits of supporting local products and services. It also showed, very clearly, the need for a marketing and advertising drive that informed all consumers about the campaign and the benefits of supporting local goods and services. The decision was also made to run the campaign through a Section 21 (non-profit company) which would facilitate its independence and ensure shared ownership by the four constituencies.

The core target audience for Proudly South African was *all* South Africans, but three distinct phases were formulated and each phase actively focused on specific core markets. Firstly, business, media, community structures, organized labour and government; secondly, South African consumers and thirdly, international consumers, tourists and export stakeholders.

The objectives of the campaign were also formulated post-research:

Primary Objective:
- To safeguard current jobs and stimulate job creation by generating demand for locally made products.

Secondary Objectives:
- To improve the quality of locally manufactured goods.
- To promote fair labour standards to protect the rights of the workers.
- To ensure environmentally responsible management practices.
- To promote the use of local inputs (local content).

The campaign objectives are very simple in nature yet in practice proved more challenging and complicated. In order for PSA to achieve these objectives substantial capital was necessary to launch the campaign and to ensure it would become self-sustainable. The initial funding for the campaign was to be sourced from the social partners: government through the Department of Trade and Industry, business through major sponsors and community and labour through contributions 'in kind'. With the role of Government in the economy being marginalized, the need for 'anchor sponsors' was also identified to ensure a steady income stream during the early years. As a result the PSA Founder Sponsor Programme, essentially an innovative cause-related marketing opportunity, was developed as a co-operative marketing venture between the public and private sectors.

The premise of the programme was to source additional revenue for PSA, through endorsement from leading blue-chip brands and additional marketing and communication activities around the PSA brand. In return, PSA would provide founder sponsors with a package of unique benefits that they could in turn utilize to build and position their own brands and drive sales of their products and services.

The founder sponsors all sought to accomplish their own specific objectives, but simultaneously, in order to ultimately achieve the objectives set out in terms of the overall campaign. The Founder Sponsor programme also established a number of sponsorship and other marketing opportunities for PSA to achieve its business objectives.

The design of the programme was such that five major South African companies, desiring to be associated with the Proudly South African initiative, provided the initial income. The five respected, well-known, aspirational brands would also be positioned with a brand whose defining characteristics engender emotional equity from the target markets, in particular pride, patriotism, commitment and passion. This association contractually binds the company to leverage their association with the campaign at least 1:1.

Leading on from this, the Founder Sponsor programme created sponsorship opportunities for PSA to achieve its business objectives whilst providing the founder sponsor companies with an opportunity to be associated with an extremely credible cause, namely job creation. It also provided an opportunity to achieve effective product differentiation by using the Proudly South African trademark and thereby gaining a competitive advantage from the trademark's endorsement by linking the founder sponsor's own products to the trademark attributes. This would give consumers confidence and would help to sway buying behaviour and create the opportunity for the founder sponsor company and its products and services to be identified as being of a superior quality.

The results from the campaign, which recently celebrated its first anniversary, are overwhelming. Within the first three months of operation the PSA Founder Sponsor programme had secured four dedicated members, Old Mutual (financial services institution), Telkom (integrated communications operator), South African Airways (airline company) and Eskom (electricity and energy supplier). Barloworld (industrial brand management company) later joined as the final founder sponsor. To date the PSA Founder Sponsor Programme has raised its target amount of R99 million, in cash and 'value in kind' through sponsor leveraging activities, over their three year contracts.

The PSA Campaign has secured over 1100 members to date and the total media value gained from the various communications channels amounts to over R100 million, compared to the actual spend by PSA of just over R15 million. The instantaneous success of the PSA Campaign can be attributed to the dedication of the four constituencies involved and the professional manner in which this non-profit company has been managed. The initiation of the PSA Founder Sponsor programme ensured the necessary funding was immediately available and the programme created a platform to generate mass awareness for the campaign and so accruing additional revenue streams through increased membership and public support. In addition PSA has embarked upon a well executed marketing campaign which has included a national outdoor billboard campaign as well as 'PSA Day' whereby members were encouraged to get staff behind the cause by asking them to demonstrate their commitment to Proudly South African campaign in various ways on that day.

Figure 5.8 Proudly South African Logo. Reprinted with permission from Proudly South African

KEY INSIGHT

Acknowledging different needs of the public and private sector yet working together to develop a meaningful campaign with mutually beneficial objectives resulted in the success of this cause-related marketing initiative. The campaign also appeals to all South Africans so gaining buy-in from the relevant constituencies and individuals was an integral part of the success.

City Partnerships

Opportunities also exist to partner Cities either by way of co-operating around the staging of events and/or activities or, as the City of London recently showed, by way of branding throughout the city. In what has been labelled as the first commercial sponsorship of a capital city, Partners for London plans to raise £150 million over the next ten years from sponsors in 20 different categories to make London a cleaner and more attractive place to do business. HSBC were the first sponsor to take up the offer for a reported £40 million over four years that has seen the bank's logo displayed on all manner of places throughout the City including for example the airbridges at Heathrow Airport. Anyone that has travelled recently to London will have witnessed the HSBC presence very visibly.

Passion branding in the public domain

The last opportunity that I wanted to touch on was that of passion branding in the public domain.

In certain situations, the opportunity may exist for a brand to take 'ownership' of an event or a special occasion that is not otherwise technically owned by anyone; New Year's Eve for example. The beauty of these types of associations is that the brand's budget can be allocated in full towards leveraging the association of the brand with the event or activity without being diluted by rights fees or 'license' fees normally associated with a sponsorship. The down-side of course is that you have no protection against any other brand deciding to use the event or special occasion as a marketing platform, including a competitor. As a sponsor of, for example, a sports event or federation, this protection would be afforded you.

As in all passion branding activities, the success of this approach will be linked directly to the relevance between the event or activity and the brand concerned. A great example of where this approach has worked is that of Guinness and St. Patrick's Day, as Diageo's Sean O'Neill explains.

Leading Thought
Sean O'Neill, *Brand and Market Communication Director, Diageo*

In the minds of consumers around the world and in terms of beer, Guinness is synonymous with St. Patrick's Day. We recognize that this gives us a significant opportunity – particularly in certain markets like the US and Australia where Irish heritage is really important – to use this as an experiential platform for consumers.

Understanding what is important to consumers is critical to success on St. Patrick's Day. If all we did was to play on our Irish heritage and our Irish credentials, we would very, very quickly be seen only as an Irish beer.

Guinness has been involved with St. Patrick's Day for literally as long as it has been a significant global celebration. A hundred years ago, the concept of a St. Patrick's Day celebration meant that Irish people around the world would celebrate in their traditional Irish way which was, in part, through drinking Guinness. We have always been very proud of the fact that Irish people around the world drank Guinness on St. Patrick's Day and also that the people who felt they wanted to be Irish, or who claimed some Irishness, would drink Guinness because of that.

But, you know, St. Patrick's Day is a fantastic showcase for the brand and as such a great trial and recruitment opportunity. So, increasingly, we are looking to give consumers a brilliant contemporary Guinness experience on St. Patrick's Day.

Our challenge though is to do this without losing the Irish feel. How do you ensure that you're promoting things other than your Irish heritage because you know that the consumer finds more than that relevant about the brand? How do you build in contemporary Irishness? How do you link in local treatments? How do you explain that Guinness is first a brilliant beer and secondly a fantastic global brand? How do you use it to reflect and deepen consumers' understanding of our key brand benefit? Those are the challenges of St. Patrick's Day.

Combining passion branding platforms for maximum impact

Opportunities often exist to combine two or more passion branding platforms, e.g. cause-related and sports marketing, as we saw earlier with Old Mutual's Save Chapman's Peak Fund and the Two Oceans Marathon, or social responsibility and sports marketing as demonstrated by Laureus.

The benefits of using a high profile activity like sport to attract the attention of fans as a lever for other 'soft' initiatives are numerous as HSBC have shown with the HSBC Global Education Challenge.

CASE STUDY

HSBC Global Education Challenge

HSBC Group is one of the world's largest banking and financial services organizations with 32 million customers and 170,000 employees in 81 countries and territories. The Group is a multi-local organization; on the ground, and part of the local culture in over 81 countries. The brand represents the belief in a balance of local understanding and global leadership, the belief that good ideas and practices in money-management can come from anywhere.

Key to HSBC's corporate social responsibility strategy is the belief that support for primary and secondary education is crucial to the future development and prosperity of every country. It is for this reason, that the Group invests in excess of US$11 million each year on education projects worldwide and has supported education initiatives for many years.

With the establishment of HSBC's UK Education Trust, and subsequent research into HSBC's global education projects, it became clear that internal and external awareness of the Group's education activities was lacking. For this reason, HSBC sought a sponsorship property which would fulfil the dual role of raising awareness of HSBC's support of education and providing a valuable educational resource for children around the world. In selecting an appropriate sponsorship, HSBC needed a global property which could carry the brand to a global audience in line with HSBC's major markets. In addition, HSBC wanted something that leant itself to communication via the internet as this was in keeping with its brand positioning and would also ensure extensive reach and facilitate greater interaction.

HSBC identified the Around Alone yacht race as a suitable sponsorship platform and became the primary sponsor of Graham Dalton and his yacht, Hexagon, for the 2002/03 race. Around Alone is one of the toughest sporting challenges known to man and involves solo sailors circumnavigating the globe, covering 28,000 nautical miles. The race is an excellent source of information on the environment, geography, weather, culture and technology and, therefore, provides an enormous amount of educational material for children. Sailing as a sport has a high degree of statistical interest, is ideal for web communication as it is very visual, and it is 24/7, so it can work across time zones. The race is truly global with stopover ports in New York, Torbay (UK), Cape Town (South Africa), Tauranga (New Zealand), Salvador da Bahia (Brazil), and Newport (USA), thereby, providing HSBC with a high-profile global opportunity to tell the HSBC education story and leverage the sponsorship in a number of its key territories. Graham Dalton has shown a commitment to improving children's education opportunities through sport and thus HSBC's interactive education programme, the HSBC Global Education Challenge, made perfect sense. The *Hexagon* skipper aptly sums up what the sponsorship is all about when he says – '*Hexagon* is not a boat, it is a banner for education, a rallying point for education. Without the education integrated into our race, it wouldn't be a worthwhile project. We [Graham Dalton and HSBC] share this common vision.'

The HSBC Global Education Challenge is primarily targeted at children between the ages of 9 and 12 years as well as a wider audience of HSBC staff and customers and sailing enthusiasts. In creating the programme, HSBC hoped to achieve the following objectives:

- Communicate and raise awareness around HSBC's support for education both internally and externally.
- Help raise funds for local education projects.
- Provide a free, internet-based learning tool for children to use from home and for teachers to supplement their curriculum activities.

HSBC launched the HSBC Global Education Challenge, a US$1 million investment in online education, in September 2002. Children wishing to participate in the 32 weekly stimulating and exciting challenges themed around the race, register online, complete the exercises and enter their answers into their own personal ship's logbook. Thereafter, they are rewarded with a 'treasure chest' of fun activities for having completed a module. Because the programme is internet-based, it allows for flexible participation – children either participate as part of a school curriculum or in their own time at home. The challenges also require them to undertake their own research, both on-line and off-line, thereby increasing their learning.

The HSBC Global Education Challenge website also contains a number of other fun activities and interesting information on the race such as photographs, short video clips, and updates from the Hexagon skipper. In

Figure 5.9 The HSBC-sponsored yacht, *Hexagon*. Reprinted with permission from HSBC

addition, children can e-mail Graham and each week a selection of e-mails and his responses are featured on the site.

To leverage the sponsorship, HSBC has initiated a number of activities such as:

- School tours showing children around *Hexagon*.
- School visits and motivational speeches by Graham Dalton.
- Advertising in specialist teachers and parent publications.
- Customer fundraising dinners (partnering with local education charities/causes).
- Customer sailing trips on *Hexagon*.
- Exhibitions, demonstrations and hospitality at each stop over port.
- Merchandizing.
- Staff communications and competitions via the intranet and internal publications.
- Online promotions.
- Website links to other HSBC supported education programmes.

The success of the sponsorship, which is due to come to a close when the race ends in April 2003, is being measured in the following ways:

Figure 5.10 Skipper Graham Dalton with children on the Global Challenge Programme. Reprinted with permission from HSBC

Figure 5.11 St. Joseph's School pupils participating in the HSBC Global Education Challenge Programme. Reprinted with permission from HSBC

- Monitoring the number of registered users of the online education programme and the amount of time they spend on the site.
- Monitoring the number of repeat visits to the sailing site.
- Global press coverage in each of HSBC's key markets.

Results so far are promising.

- The site has over 50,000 users, of which over 4,400 have registered for regular updates or to use the education programme. Over 1,800 of those registered are teachers. Users spend an average of nine minutes on the site and originate from 30 countries, with the majority from the UK, USA and New Zealand.
- In the UK alone, the value of media coverage received so far is almost £0.5m.
- The site has received great feedback from teachers and pupils. Janet Bradley, teacher of children with learning difficulties at Chamberlayne Park School, Southampton – 'I can't believe what it has done to the kids, especially those who are usually very negative about their work. They forget their learning difficulties and get on with accessing information.'

KEY INSIGHT

HSBC's Global Education Challenge is an excellent example of how a high profile global sponsorship such as the Around Alone yacht race can be extended to incorporate another of the sponsoring company's key strategic thrusts, in this case education. By using the Around Alone yacht race, HSBC is able to generate global interest and awareness of its education initiatives whilst also creating an interesting, fun and exciting learning environment for children.

6

Strategic passion branding
management

We now turn our attention to the ever important process of bringing life to the discipline of passion branding in a structured and informed framework that will ensure that you, as a passion brander, will deliver against your business goals and vision.

Passion branding road map

With a focus on effect-driven, as opposed to output-driven, sponsorships the passion branding road map is designed in such a way as to bring a degree of process to what has traditionally been a very 'loose' discipline. The focus on effect is very important. There is no point in going down the passion branding route unless you are convinced that your efforts are going to make a meaningful contribution towards achieving your business and communication objectives.

At the end of the day, passion branding should set out to achieve business and communication objectives. The passion branding road map set out below provides a framework within which passion branders can manage the process of delivering against these objectives in an accountable manner whilst not limiting the strategic creativity required of an effective passion branding campaign.

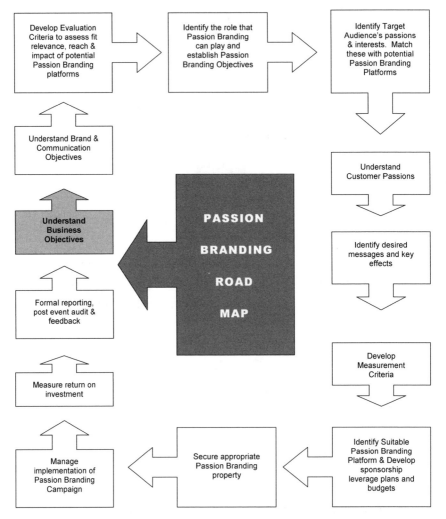

Figure 6.1 Passion branding road map

Understand Business Objectives

Q: What is it that the business is trying to achieve and what role could passion branding potentially play in this regard?

A real understanding of the business in which the brand operates is an essential starting point for any successful passion branding campaign. This includes an understanding of the entire value chain from production through to distribution and sales with a view to identifying the potential connections with stakeholders that could be made through the campaign.

The current business environment is equally important. Identify any challenges and/or opportunities that the business might find itself faced with and highlight those that a passion branding campaign may be able to influence. These might include things like a new entrant to the market, changing legislation and changing customer preferences.

It also pays at this stage to gain an understanding of competitor activity within the category both in terms of product attributes, challenges and opportunities, brand positioning and communication activities being undertaken by the brand.

At the end of this phase, informed by a good understanding of the business, the passion brander should be fully attuned with the specific business objectives at hand and should have started to get a feel for the general role that sponsorship can play in helping to achieve these objectives.

Understand brand and communication objectives

Q: In respect of the lead brand to be used in the potential passion branding campaign what are the key messages that need to be communicated around the brand?

Understand the brand from a strategic perspective including the key brand benefit (or unique selling proposition), brand identity and its positioning along with all other relevant brand attributes. These will be played back through the passion branding campaign so a thorough understanding of these elements is crucial.

Q: Have you developed sufficient insight into the brand's target audience in terms of their passions and interests?

Gather as much information about the brand's customers and stakeholders with a view to gaining insight into their demographics and psychographics, likes and dislikes, passions and interests. This insight will play a major role in determining which passion branding platform is most appropriate for your brand.

Develop evaluation criteria that check sponsorship platforms for fit, relevance, impact, reach and behavioural change

Q: Have you developed an evaluation template against which you can objectively assess all passion branding opportunities?

Before you delve into the detail of constructing your passion branding campaign, it pays to have developed a set of evaluation criteria against which you can assess and compare potential passion branding opportunities.

These criteria should be as objective as possible and should address at least the following elements:

- *Fit or relevance* between your brand and its target audience and the passion branding platform under consideration.
- The potential *impact* of the campaign on the fans; will they notice it and will it capture their attention?
- The *quantity, quality and location of fans* that the platform provides access to and where. What type of media do the platform's fans consume and how?
- The *degree of passion* displayed by the platform's fans and the extent to which this passion can be harnessed and converted into benefits for the sponsoring brand, e.g., loyalty towards the sponsoring brand.
- The platform's fans *attitude* towards sponsoring brands.
- The extent to which the platform can contribute towards enhancing the sponsoring brand's *brand image and attributes* such as its key brand benefit, positioning, values and messages.
- Opportunities for the sponsoring brand to deliver *a unique brand experience* for the fans.
- The extent to which the platform can *generate business opportunities* and drive *incremental sales* of the sponsoring brand.

- The *track record* of the platform owners and/or organizers. Do they have a reputation for delivery?
- The platform's *hygiene factors* including its history, involvement of co-sponsors, potential risks associated with the platform, political or legislative issues.
- The *scope of the rights package* being offered and the extent to which an association with the platform can be *leveraged*.
- *Resources* required to ensure the success of the campaign including rights fee, leverage budget, staffing and political will within the company to make it work.
- *Measurement criteria* and targets used to assess the success of the campaign.
- The sponsoring brands *relevance* within the context of the platform.

Given the nature of passion branding, the best evaluation criteria are those that call for written motivation or comment in respect of each area of the evaluation as opposed to a simple, or even complicated, numerical scoring methodology. At this stage of the process, having been given all the facts, the passion brander should be guided by their better judgement as to the suitability of a passion platform rather than their ability to assign and add a set of numbers.

Identify the role that passion branding can play and establish passion branding objectives

Q: Given the business, brand and communication objectives, is there a role for passion branding or could these objectives be better met through some other marketing or communication effort? If passion branding is considered relevant, what are the objectives of the passion branding campaign?

Passion branding may not always be the most relevant form of communication available to a marketer and it is important to establish as early on as possible whether passion branding has the capability to achieve the business, brand and communication objectives at hand. Passion branding does some things better than other forms of communication but, when used in isolation, it is limited in some areas so be very clear as to what it is that you are trying to achieve.

Set the objectives against what the property must deliver. They should ideally be specific, measurable, achievable, relevant and timed.

The most effective passion branding campaigns are those where the passion branding campaign is used as a central theme of all brand communication.

Leading Thought
Sean O'Neill, *Brand and Market Communication Director, Diageo*

The role of sponsorship is to help us grow our brands – pure and simple. It can do this in a huge number of ways – either through building the image dimensions of a brand, delivering awareness, changing perceptions as well as the very obvious route of increasing sales. The hard part is knowing exactly the role you want sponsorship to play in the mix, what clear objectives you want it to achieve and why you are using sponsorship to achieve these as opposed to another discipline.

There's a whole heap of people out there like me, who would watch a big sporting event even if it wasn't their sport of choice but it's a connection moment nonetheless for a consumer simply because it's a big sporting event.

For example, the Rugby World Cup is one of the world's top four sporting events. In the UK and Ireland we wanted to use the sponsorship to drive incremental volume amongst existing drinkers (who we knew would be watching) and also – on a secondary basis – to recruit new drinkers into the brand who would be watching the event because of its size rather than because it was rugby.

In the southern hemisphere, our aims were the same, but reversed in terms of importance because the sport has a high penetration and relevance amongst our target consumers.

Identify the target audience's passions and interests and match these with potential passion branding platforms

Q: Have you developed sufficient insight into possible passion branding platforms with a view to establishing a relevant match with the brand's target audience?

The starting point for any successful passion branding campaign is to ensure the right fit between the passion platform, its fans and the sponsoring brand. In order to do this, the passion brander needs to have an in depth understanding of the potential passion branding platform and its fans, both demographically and attitudinally.

There is generally a dearth of demographic information available in the traditional passion branding platforms – such as sport, for example – and there also tends to be only a limited amount of attitudinal information available on the open market in respect of most platforms. As a result, it would seem that the majority of decisions being made today as to which platform is most appropriate for a passion branding campaign are still essentially based on a 'gut feeling'.

Passion branders should invest both the resources and the time required in order to gain a better understanding of the attitudes of the fans that they hope to be able to influence through their passion branding campaigns before concluding on the appropriateness, or otherwise, of the platform that they have identified. This should be done up-front before any decision is taken as to which platform may be most appropriate and before any commitment is made.

The best passion branding campaigns are those that demonstrate the greatest relevance, or fit, between the passion platform's fans and those of the sponsoring brand. The selection of passion branding platforms based on the personal preferences of the company Chairman or Marketing Director should be discouraged.

Understanding customers' passions

Although it does still happen, albeit at a much lower level than has historically been the case, the days of a company or brand becoming involved in a passion platform at the whim of the Chairman are over.

As the level of sophistication applied by marketers in the ambit of sponsorship marketing increases – and the marketing department, as opposed to the Chairman's office, becomes responsible for the selection and management of a company or a brand's sponsorship activities – so the rigours of traditional marketing start to be applied to sponsorship.

Words like 'reach', 'frequency', 'target-audience' – previously foreign to sponsorship practitioners – are fast becoming part of the everyday language of passion branders. And as marketers start to understand the potential power of passion branding as a business and communication tool, so too do they start to realize that the level of insight into the fans that they are hoping to reach and influence through their sponsorship campaigns is limited.

There seems to be very little off-the-shelf attitudinal research available when it comes to passion platforms and their fans. Yes, you can quite easily find out a whole range of demographic information about passion platforms and their fans but try and scratch the surface and you will likely come up empty-handed. So, it is possible to match a company or brand demographically to a passion platform and its fans but it requires a lot more effort and money to be able to make an attitudinal fit.

A client described it well recently when describing the typical approach at a consumer focus group at their company. 'We'll ask a consumer what sport they play. They'll reply golf and then we'll move on to the next question without further interrogating what golf means to that consumer, how passionate they are about golf, how they consume their golf, what their attitudes are towards sponsors of golf, how they think sponsors of golf should be interacting with golfers and what they should be doing for golf'.

Effective matching of 'brands to fans' requires insight into the demographic and attitudinal factors associated with both the sponsoring brand and the passion platform and its fans. And it should be researched in advance and not left to 'gut feeling' alone which is so often the case.

Leading Thought
Chuck Fruit, *Senior Vice President, The Coca-Cola Company*

Sponsorship provides not only a very effective platform to define the character, personality, and values of a brand, but I believe it also provides an implied endorsement for the brand from a 'trusted friend.' For example, if a consumer is passionate about soccer, and Coca-Cola is woven into the fabric of soccer, then there can be a transfer of the emotional attachment over to the brand – a kind of endorsement from soccer that is difficult to evoke through traditional forms of advertising.

For me, the key to achieving great exploitation comes right back to understanding the consumer, simply because if you know the connection points and you know what the consumer is interested in doing, and is prepared to do, you can shape every single aspect of the exploitation plan around that.

Identify the key effects desired and messages to be conveyed through the passion branding campaign

Q: What effect do you want the passion branding campaign to have on your brand and business?

Q: What change in consumer behaviour do you want to bring about as a result of the passion branding campaign?

Having satisfied yourself that passion branding does provide a suitable vehicle through which your business, brand and communication objectives can be met, you will need to decide on the key effect that you want to have as a result of the campaign. This might include things such as enhancing customer attitudes towards your brand, e.g., an increased level of trust in the brand or increasing purchase consideration of your brand. If you have identified up front what factor it is that you specifically want to move the needle against then you will find it all the more easier to shape your passion branding activities with these objectives in mind.

At all costs, avoid the trap of trying to use the campaign to achieve every objective under the sun for this will stretch your budget and resources and will certainly undermine the potential of the campaign to achieve what it is best positioned to achieve.

Q: What are the key messages that you want to communicate through the sponsorship?

The same applies to the brand messages that you wish to convey through the campaign. Identify the key messages that you believe can best be conveyed through the campaign and stick relentlessly to this message throughout.

Develop measurement criteria, methodology and benchmarks

Q: How will you establish whether the campaign has achieved its objectives or not?

I have sat in many a company Board meeting where half the directors believe the campaign should continue and the other half would like to see it in the trash can. At the end of the day, the group that carries the greatest political influence determines whether the campaign lives or dies; surely not the best way to evaluate anything.

By establishing measurement criteria at this stage of the process, in advance of any implementation, as well as benchmarks for success, the subjectivity so often seen in such evaluations can be removed and replaced with a greater degree of objectivity and most importantly accountability.

All stakeholders that will be involved in any decision making around the campaign should also buy into these criteria and benchmarks in advance.

Identify a suitable passion branding platform and develop sponsorship leverage plans and budgets

Q: Have you identified a suitable platform and have all the potential leverage opportunities connected to the platform been identified? Is there sufficient budget available to fully exploit these opportunities?

There is little point in spending your entire budget securing a passion platform only to then realize that you have insufficient funds to fully leverage the property. You would be surprised how many marketers are still guilty of this cardinal sin!

Once you have identified what it is that you want to achieve with your campaign and you have identified (NB not secured – that comes later) a suitable passion platform for this purpose, you should develop the various leverage opportunities connected to the platform and determine the budgets that will be required in order to fully exploit these opportunities.

Develop the key leverage themes and integrate into these the key messages that need to be communicated through the platform.

Q: Do you have the necessary resources required to effectively leverage the property?

You should also at this stage of the process identify what resources you will utilize to actually implement the passion branding campaign. These could be in-house resources or alternatively the services of a specialist passion branding agency or some combination thereof. In determining how best to resource such a project, consideration should be given to the capabilities that you will require and the associated costs.

Secure appropriate passion property

Q: Is it more appropriate to utilize an existing passion platform, e.g. World Cup Soccer, or create one that you, as the brand, can own, develop and manage to suit your own specific needs.

It is important to highlight the fact that it is only at this stage of the process that you should go about actually securing the passion property that you have identified, and no sooner. By approaching things in this order you will have ensured that the passion platform that you have identified is the most appropriate one for you and also that you have sufficient funds available to secure both the necessary rights and, more importantly, the capacity to leverage the passion property at the level required in order to achieve your objectives.

Should you decide to go the route of associating with an existing passion platform, then before committing to the passion platform identified it is important that you carry out a detailed review of the platform and its owners to ensure that there are no skeletons in the cupboard that may come back to haunt you at a later stage. As I discuss later in this chapter, it is easier to strike up an association with a passion platform than it is to get out of one so satisfy yourself that you are doing the right thing before signing on the dotted line.

Alternatively, should you opt to go the route of creating your own passion branding platform, you will need to consider how best to go about establishing such a platform in as low a risk environment as possible. It may often pay to involve a specialized agency in such instances as the right agency will be able to help you manage your risk to an acceptable level while also giving you a degree of comfort *vis-à-vis* the final delivery of the platform.

Leading Thought
Sean O'Neill, *Brand and Market Communication Director, Diageo*

My honest belief is that the biggest challenge is for marketers to understand our consumer a hundred times better than we do now – their passions and what makes them tick; then, on the basis of that understanding, we need to discover how best to reach and connect with them. And, whilst I know that is the essence of marketing that I've just described, I don't believe marketing as a discipline, yet focuses enough on the consumer.

I also believe that there's a particular relevance in this for sponsorship. Sponsorship should be a triangular relationship between the brand, the event or property you're sponsoring and the consumer. Too often, only two of these three dimensions are considered, and for a sponsorship to truly deliver, it has to work across all 3 dimensions, with particular focus on the consumer relationship to the brand and the property. If you can establish a clear triangular relationship then you're absolutely right to really consider that particular sponsorship.

We're in business to sell our brands. We're not in business to grow or promote a sport. Taking the values of a given sport on the basis that they have significance and very high relevance and resonance with our consumers is essentially why we undertake sponsorships.

Ultimately, we believe that we can, through the association, drive growth on a particular brand provided we can engage our consumers in the activity. This means that our target consumer has to have a passion for whatever we are sponsoring. A passing interest alone isn't enough.

So finding a property or a platform in which your consumer has a real passion, and which is highly relevant to them in their life, is potentially a huge connection moment. Then, working out a clever and powerful way of exploiting that passion through the sponsorship is essential.

Q: Have the rights and obligations of all parties involved in the campaign been clearly identified in a legally binding contract?

You only need a contract when things go wrong, so make sure at this early stage of your relationship with the property owner or other third parties that may be involved such as a specialist agency, media owners, athletes, etc., that you have covered all eventualities in a legally binding agreement signed by all parties. This agreement will play an important role in regulating the relationships around the campaign and the basis upon which various parties are required to deliver so it is worthwhile investing in the services of a professional lawyer in drawing up the agreement. Given the specialized nature of such agreements, consideration should be given to professionals that have the relevant experience and expertise in the area.

Manage the implementation of the passion branding campaign

Q: Have you developed a detailed implementation plan that sets out the 'how', 'what', 'where' and 'when' with regards to the implementation of the passion branding campaign.

Now it is time to roll up your sleeves and get down to the dirty work of making it all happen. Notice how far we are along the process before we get down to actually doing the thing! This is important as many people's natural instinct is to start doing before they start thinking which results in lots of hard work but not necessarily anything to show for it.

You should ask yourself over and over during the implementation phase this one simple question, 'what effect is this going to have on my brand and/ or my business?' If the answer does not relate specifically back to the key effects identified earlier in the process then you should not be doing whatever it is that you're considering.

As the passion brander, your responsibility is to leverage your brand's association with the passion platform and not to actually take responsibility for managing the platform itself, which is the responsibility of the platform owner or organizer. Beware the risks of getting sucked into the detail of the platform itself as this will prove to be nothing more than a distraction. Having said this, you need to keep a watchful eye on the organizers to ensure that they deliver a successful event that will add to, rather than distract from, your brand and business.

Measure return on investment against pre-determined criteria

Q: How is the campaign performing?

I am a great believer in ongoing measurement as the information that this provides you with can be used as a great management tool to regulate your activities and areas of focus. It is all very well finding out at the end of a campaign that it did or did not achieve its objectives but rather more useful finding this out during the campaign and having the opportunity to correct things where they might not be going according to plan.

The involvement of independent third parties in this process can also be useful as it provides an impartial and objective assessment but be cautious when making use of inflexible off-the-shelf measurement tools as these may restrict your ability to measure what is really important.

On completion of the campaign, the various pre-determined measurement criteria need to be evaluated and compared against benchmarks established up front.

Formal reporting, post-event audit and feedback

Q: Has the passion branding campaign achieved its pre-determined objectives?

Given that measurement criteria and benchmarks have been set up front, this should be a simple yes or no.

All relevant stakeholders should be updated post-campaign as to the results achieved and given the opportunity to assess for themselves whether the campaign has been a success or not.

The facts should speak for themselves and the fact that the passion brander has been prepared to be held accountable for the results of the campaign greatly enhance the relationship between the passion brander and these stakeholders.

Q: In what areas could we have done better and how could we improve in these areas?

Based on the learnings from the campaign, develop recommendations for the next cycle to ensure that the same mistakes are not repeated.

Q: Should we continue to invest in the passion branding platform in the future?

At the conclusion of this process at the end of a campaign's cycle, the passion brander will have come full circle and should go back to the beginning of the process before attempting to answer this question.

The elements of a successful passion branding programme

Thought leaders within the industry have some useful advice when it comes to highlighting the elements of a successful sponsorship.

Leading Thought
Chuck Fruit, *Senior Vice President, The Coca-Cola Company*

We have a very shorthand way of thinking about sponsorships: buy only what you need; use what you buy; and measure the results.

'Buy only what you need' implies the necessity of understanding the business purpose of a sponsorship and the specific role the sponsorship will play in your business or brand building activities.

Then 'use what you buy' means that all of the possible applications of the sponsorship must be exploited (from a promotional stand point, from retail customer building opportunities, community involvement, employee opportunities), and it also implies a commitment to creatively activate your involvement.

And then 'measure the results' is one of the easiest things to neglect, as you know. Sometimes, after a sponsorship has been completed, the tendency is to 'declare victory' and move on to the next sponsorship, rather than to pause, measure and reflect on what we learned.

Leading Thought
Michael Brockbank, *Vice President Brand Communication, Unilever*

Our advertising is rooted in consumer understanding and original insights. Equally true for sponsorship – except that sponsorship must tap into the real passions of consumers – things they feel much more strongly about than their washing powder or their mayonnaise. So we must understand what they think, and what they feel. And realize how much harm we can do to our brand's relationship with its consumers if we get their passions wrong, if we misunderstand them, mistreat them, or drop our support of them from one moment to the next.

Our advertising contains strong, distinctive ideas – equally true again, except in sponsorship we need to have great ideas at three different levels. We need to choose the right category of activities, like marathon running, or fashion or road safety. We need to find a great idea for an activity that communicates our brand within that category. And we need ideas for execution and implementation that will bring the sponsorship to life for the consumer, and maximize the value of our investment.

Our advertising involves and delights the consumer – equally true for sponsorship. Except if we are involving and delighting them, we had better take into account how they react when we stop doing so or do it badly. We are soon forgiven if we stop a much-loved advertising campaign; generally another one comes along soon.

Everything that we do in sponsorship is required to be brand and consumer-led and categorically not property led. Our sponsorship must leverage consumer passion, and in order to do that we must have real insight into that passion.

At the most important moments of the process, the points of decision, the 'go/no go' moments, we ask our colleagues to think less about the look on their own face as they present the trophy, or on their admiring partner's face, or on their chairman's face, or even on his partner's face … and more about the look on their consumers' faces as they watch or take part in the sponsored activity, about the thoughts and feelings which go through consumers in understanding the role our brand has played in bringing the activity to them.

We bring our belief in brand value migration to every aspect of our sponsorship, and we understand that there has to be mutual value for us, for the activity and for the consumer.

We want our brands to stand out, but not at all costs, as we know that what was once regarded as an appropriate branded presence now runs the risk of being seen as commercial pollution if the value to the consumer is not clear.

We are led by a tight brief, developed by a tight team, and we insist that our marketers don't rely on agencies that own or sell rights in the development of that brief.

The right sponsorship for us does not have to be good. It has to be great. It has to fulfil our 'abc criteria' for effective communication, as we don't think sponsorship works any differently to anything else. We won't escape advertising clutter only to find ourselves in sponsorship clutter. Less is more, for us, and we look for partners who share that view.

We identify a short list of big ideas. But our decision on which one we choose is never based on personal preference and isn't based on the brilliance of a sales pitch. We always take our ideas back to the consumer, as what seems like a good idea to us might not resonate with them. We explore whether it inspires them, convinces them, makes them think any differently of us.

We plan our leverage right up front, and if we find that we don't have enough resources or enough imagination to truly bring our preferred idea to life, we choose another.

We always judge our sponsorship in terms of outcome rather than output. Knowing that (and I quote) 'television coverage of motor racing's Formula One World Championship was watched by 54.5 billion viewers last year' tells us nothing. I wonder on which planet the 46.5 billion who've escaped the earth's population statistics live.

Who cares? We want to know in what way did our sponsorship affect a change in the behaviour of our consumers.

Only once we've thoroughly analysed, and understood the value of the sponsorship to us do we come to the table and negotiate the deal. And given our unease over the transparency in the industry, be aware that we are scrupulous in our due diligence.

Leading Thought
Sally Hancock, *Chief Executive, Redmandarin*

Consumer insight is vital – to know the target audience, to know their interest, to know the way that they're going to consume your brand through this activity, to know the way that you're going to create memorable meeting points through this activity.

The brand has to be the starting base along with consumer insight. Only once that is determined and a strategy is devised, should a sponsor then go and either look for properties that fit that or create their own. More often than not it's about piecing together and combining together different things to make a whole.

Then there's activation – if you don't fully integrate sponsorship it's like buying a poster site and leaving it blank, so integration is critical. In the States, Coca-Cola now say that the ratio of their activation budget to rights fees is about 8:1 – although it's more important to determine the right level of activation to meet the objectives of the sponsorship than worry about ratios.

And finally the need to take a partnership approach. The most effective sponsorship contracts tend to be longer term, with flexibility in the contract. It's important to understand the needs of both parties and to look for a win-win solution for both parties.

We tend to think that about 90 per cent of sponsorship budgets are wasted because they're either not strategic or there's no intent or purpose defined, there's no effective evaluation, or the sponsorship is not integrated. All of these contribute to making it effective.

Extracting maximum value through leverage programmes

The most successful passion branding campaigns are those that place the passion platform at the heart of brand building and use it as a platform off which a myriad of communication activities are launched.

There are no limits to the possibilities when passion branding is approached in this manner with the sponsorship providing the central theme to all communication activities and being truly integrated into every aspect of the sponsors business.

Common wisdom has it that effective sponsorship programmes require that for every US$1 spent directly on a securing sponsorship rights, between US$1 and US$3 should be spent leveraging those rights through other forms of support communication. Whatever the ratio, the principle of leveraging your direct sponsorship spend with additional support spend holds true and is a factor that should be incorporated within every sponsorship campaign.

Leading Thought
Chris Weil, *Chairman and Chief Executive, Momentum Worldwide*

Done properly, sponsorship is part of the marketing mix and acts as an anchor for full through-the-line communication. Too many times people buy the sponsorship and say 'okay, I've got my boards up there and I've got my hospitality' and then at the end that say 'gosh, this was expensive'. The reality however is that sponsorship should be the core of the idea, but that's only the starting point. From there, all of the communications needs to be developed around the sponsorship.

I always say, where people often go wrong in the marketing side is that brands are not what marketers say they are – brands are what consumers believe they are. Our job as marketers then is to orchestrate the consumer brand experience in such a way that they come to the right conclusion.

Advertising – TV, radio, print

TV, radio and print advertising have an important part to play in any integrated passion branding campaign, in amplifying the key messages being conveyed by the sponsorship itself beyond the limits of the direct environs of the platform itself, e.g. event venue. There are only so many fans that can physically attend an event, for example, but many multiples more who are interested and can see, read or hear about the event thanks to traditional media platforms prior to, during and after the event.

The effectiveness of these forms of communication are greatly enhanced when the theme of the communication relates back to a passion that is real, not borrowed, as is so often the case with classical above-the-line advertising. Passion branding therefore provides marketers with the added benefit of increasing the effectiveness of their traditional above-the-line spend.

Media leveraging

Given its intrinsic credibility, few marketers would argue that media coverage, particularly branded coverage in which the sponsor's name and/or logo appears, is worth significantly more to a brand than traditional advertising. This applies to sponsorship-linked media coverage as much as it does to any other form of corporate media.

Passion brandings' ability to provide a platform off which relevant 'free' media can be leveraged is probably one of its strongest attributes. The range of activities utilized by an event sponsor to capitalize on this strength are diverse and can include anything from a media conference to a one-on-one photo shoot with a star athlete and includes all forms of media from electronic to print.

As with all sponsorship-related communication however, one needs to focus one's efforts on generating 'free' media that is relevant and that communicates the sponsor's key messages.

Leading Thought
Iain Banner, *Chief Executive, Laureus World Sports Awards*

It's all about the credibility of the sponsor and the sponsor's activity. Consumers are terribly aware today of what marketers are trying to do and I don't believe that by simply being present marketers can enhance, engage or harness the passion. But if they're associated with the platform and they take that platform and utilize it creatively in their communication channels, then I think they can harness it.

Too many people still rely on the eyeball count – people just seeing the brand name and identity. I think that that's under threat in the future. Indiscriminate brand presence without support will not translate; but can Shell take that platform and integrate it onto the forecourt to drive traffic and ensure that the people that come and fill up will be motivated to be loyal to Shell? Yes I believe that. Will they secure loyalty because the car's driving around with a Shell sticker on board? Probably not. It's how they use that presence. Brand presence is important and it will have a certain amount of rub-off. But it's more about the leverage; it's more about having the opportunity to leverage that presence.

Hospitality

Another key leveraging opportunity presented by most sponsorships is that of hospitality, that is, the opportunity to entertain key stakeholders making use of the passion platform, e.g. at an event.

Apart from providing an opportunity to be able to access stakeholders that might otherwise be difficult to reach, suitable hospitality provides a wonderful opportunity for a sponsoring brand to provide its guests with a unique brand experience that can positively influence their attitude towards the brand and therefore propensity to do business with the brand.

Direct Marketing

Passion platforms provide an ideal environment in which names and other details of potential customers can be collected. These 'lists' can either be provided by the platforms owners, e.g. registered or licensed road runners, or collected by the sponsoring brand using the platform as a vehicle, e.g. through a promotion linked to the platform and the campaign.

A further benefit of linking direct marketing activities to the passion platform is that they can be positioned in such a way that they are more likely to attract the attention of fans than run-of-the-mill direct marketing efforts. For example, a soccer-themed direct mail campaign by a soccer club sponsor is more likely to be considered by a fan of that same club than a non-related campaign might be, particularly where the sponsor is perceived to have genuine intentions to do good through its sponsorship of the club.

New Media – Internet, SMS

Technology can be used very effectively around passion platforms to effectively leverage a sponsoring brand's association with a platform.

This may include the use of existing new media platforms as an additional channel to consumer such as advertising on, or sponsoring, an existing internet portal directly related to the passion platform in a similar way to how one would use other forms of print and electronic media.

Alternatively, this could involve the development of a unique 'owned' new media platform for the express purpose of developing a relationship with fans and participants of the passion platform as FTSE 100 financial services group Old Mutual have done with their endurance sport portal *worldofendurance.com*. This site is used as the hub for a relationship that Old Mutual nurtures with endurance athletes by providing them with news and useful information that they can use to enhance their personal performance in various endurance sports.

The site is backed up by a weekly television series called Old Mutual's World of Endurance and a range of event sponsorships around which Old Mutual provides participants and fans with a unique Old Mutual experience. The great thing about Old Mutual's approach is that they effectively 'own' media space that they can control to a large extent in terms of the look and feel and in terms of the key messages that are conveyed.

Old Mutual also provides another great example of how technology can be used to leverage an association with a passion platform, this time road running and SMS. The benefit of SMS is that it is personal, immediate and very cost effective. Old Mutual send an SMS message to all runners in the marathons that they sponsor wishing them good luck and a safe run. This has the effect of positioning Old Mutual as a caring brand. They follow this up after the event with an SMS message of congratulations to all runners for having completed the event with a special message to those runners achieving a personal best time. In the process they have developed a very powerful relationship enhancer.

Broadcast sponsorship

Television and radio provide the greatest opportunity to amplify a sponsoring brand's association with a passion platform. This is particularly so when it comes to the actual broadcast or coverage around a passion platform.

In most cases, the owners of passion platforms have historically depended to a large extent on revenues generated from the sale of television and radio rights to broadcasters who in turn rely on the sale of advertising during and sponsorships of these broadcasts for their revenue.

As such, opportunities do exist in some markets for sponsors to associate themselves directly with such broadcasts via advertiser-funded programming as was discussed in Chapter Five.

The opportunity also exists for passion branders to take advantage of the incidental exposure opportunities around a television broadcast of a platform by way of platform signage including on-field or perimeter signage, shirt branding, etc.

The big issue with incidental exposure is, of course, clutter. As more and more advertisers make use of this opportunity so the fans tend not to notice it. As part of an integrated sponsorship strategy, signage definitely has its role to play. As a stand-alone attempt at generating awareness for your brand, I would contend that one's money could be better spent elsewhere.

Broadcasters have been known to try and cut out such signage and in such instances the passion brander needs to be one step ahead of the broadcaster in designing and locating such signage if they are to take full advantage of this opportunity.

Licensing and merchandizing

Licensing opportunities can provide an interesting platform off which to further promote a sponsoring brand's association with a passion platform and generate new revenue streams that in the right environment can actually make the sponsorship self-funding.

This is best demonstrated via a wonderful licensing programme that Octagon in South Africa were responsible for conceptualizing and co-ordinating for cellular network provider MTN. Having sponsored the MTN Gladiators for a number of years, MTN and Octagon were looking for ways to really make their investment 'sweat' both in terms of creating additional exposure for the brand but also in terms of identifying incremental revenue streams around their sponsorship. As part of their sponsorship rights package, MTN had secured the right to exploit all marks connected to MTN Gladiators.

A deal was concluded with the South African Post Office, whereby an MTN range of stamps was produced, and with fast food chain Wimpy, who ran a month long MTN Gladiators licensed promotion. Both were extremely successful – 4 million stamps were sold by the South African Post Office and Wimpy had its best grossing month ever during the promotion period. The full case study appears in Chapter Four.

Sales, trade and staff promotions

In providing a theme for a sales, trade or staff promotion, passion branding is hard to beat, particularly where the passion platform is of great interest to a wide cross-section of fans as would be the case for example around something like the Olympics or World Cup Soccer.

Everybody wants to attend these types of events but the reality is that very few can ever expect to be able to do so. Prizes affording the opportunity to attend these types of events therefore provide a great incentive to participate in the promotion.

Just think about it. As a passionate athletics fan, would you rather stand a chance to win an all-expenses once-in-a-lifetime opportunity to attend the Olympic Games in Athens as a VIP guest of Coca-Cola and be a part of history or win a seven-day vacation at a ski resort that anyone can visit any time.

It all comes down to understanding your consumers and what turns them on. If you've chosen your platform correctly then you should have something compelling to offer them.

Product sampling and demonstration

Passion platforms often provide a great opportunity for product sampling which can be restricted to certain categories of product or service. This is particularly the case where there is a degree of relevance between the product being sampled and the event itself or where the fans' experience can be enhanced in some way.

Effective leveraging

Guinness and their sponsorship of Rugby World Cup '99 provide a wonderful example of how a sponsorship should be leveraged. What makes this example even more relevant as a great example of effective leverage is the fact that Guinness had to contend with a number of other co-sponsors of the event and cut through a lot of 'sponsor noise' in order to connect with their consumers.

CASE STUDY

Guinness Rugby World Cup 1999: within a multi-sponsor event, delivering commercial goals and achieving number one sponsor status through high-profile, innovative leverage programmes

Guinness is one of the world's three truly global beer brands and, by a significant margin, the leading stout brand. In 1996, the Guinness organization had a number of key international objectives, the most important of which was to increase its market leadership in key territories through growing consumption amongst existing drinkers and attracting new drinkers. Aligning with the 1999 Rugby World Cup was seen as an excellent platform from which to achieve these goals and, in 1996, Guinness became the first of eight companies to sign up as a global sponsor and as the 'official beer' of the tournament.

This was Guinness' first truly global sponsorship and enabled the brand to reinforce its positioning as a world-class global brand through association with a high profile (the world's fourth largest sporting event) world-class event. Moreover, the reach of the event, broadcast to 135 countries, mirrored Guinness' priority markets and availability in 150 countries. The brand's core target market, male adults from legal drinking age up to around 34 years, are also keen rugby supporters.

Guinness identified the following focused, commercial outcomes from the Rugby World Cup:

- To increase consumption amongst existing drinkers in major markets – Great Britain and Ireland.
- To recruit new drinkers and achieve incremental volume growth in key growth markets – France, Australia, New Zealand, South Africa and Canada.

In order to achieve these deliverables, the company set some strategic exploitation objectives:

- To use the sponsorship as a vehicle to reinforce and build on the Guinness brand essence and to inject energy, promote newsworthiness and contemporize the brand.
- To achieve top-of-mind awareness linked to the Rugby World Cup and to be perceived as the dominant sponsor.
- To create one, consistent, global identity in terms of message, image and activity.
- To motivate and facilitate employees and business partners in all markets to exploit the sponsorship.
- To exploit everything with the sense of fun and passion which are the trademarks of the Guinness brand.

Being the first global sponsor to commit to the 1999 Rugby World Cup provided Guinness with a distinct advantage over the other sponsors in that Guinness had more time in which to activate its involvement and create a strong association with the event thereby going some way towards its objective of being perceived as the dominant sponsor which is crucial if one is to stand out in a multi-sponsor programme.

In addition, this enabled the company's markets to truly plan for and integrate activity so that the Rugby World Cup was the focus of market activity for a year rather than something which was in addition to, or did not fit with, existing plans, something which often happens with sponsorships.

The company also realized that the sponsorship would need its own structure in order to co-ordinate and drive global activity. To this end, a global steering group was formed, comprising representatives from the major participating markets and led by two project directors who split overall responsibility for different aspects of the event.

Guinness realized from the start that to truly deliver on its objectives, a substantial support budget would be required to activate the sponsorship given its spread across 40 different countries. This funding requirement was flagged and committed early. In order to ensure true focus and delivery, the majority of the support budget came from the markets with a central budget supporting creative and concept development, co-ordination and hospitality.

In order to ensure consistency across markets and maximize the benefits of the association on a global scale, a sponsorship leverage 'toolkit', containing identity manuals, promotional ideas and PR templates, was produced centrally for use by local markets. This ensured that Guinness was able to disseminate a consistent and relevant message to all markets.

The sponsorship was implemented using a variety of communication and leverage tools all of which focused on fun and the fan's experience of the Rugby World Cup.

Broadcast sponsorship

From the early consumer and return on investment research undertaken to assess the sponsorship, it was recognized early that broadcast sponsorship would be a significant and critical component of many markets' exploitation plans. Guinness negotiated a broadcast sponsorship deal in Great Britain, Ireland, South Africa, Canada and on Eurosport. It is believed that the results of a post-event survey in which Guinness achieved a 94 per cent awareness rate in the UK as a Rugby World Cup sponsor can, to a large extent, be attributed to this broadcast sponsorship deal.

Key to the positive impact of the broadcast sponsorship, was the creative and humorous execution of the broadcast elements which enhanced the viewing experience and created an emotional bond between Guinness, the viewers and the event. Stings were created and tailored to specific matches or teams. For example, when the broadcast featured a match played by the New Zealand team, otherwise known as the All Blacks, the creative treatment featured a black screen; when the French were playing, the advertising featured a cockerel on the pitch.

Signage and presence marketing

As one of the global sponsors of the competition, Guinness received perimeter boards at all matches and also negotiated additional signage at training grounds, media centres, official functions and press conferences. These additional signage opportunities helped to establish Guinness as the dominant sponsor of the competition. Guinness though went further. The early sign-up to the event, coupled with the integration of the sponsorship into the Great Britain marketing plan meant that the highest profile outdoor and mobile sites around each major venue were purchased in advance, which added significantly to the Guinness presence around the event.

Promotions

Both off-trade and on-trade promotions, conducted in all priority markets, were a key leverage tool used by Guinness to encourage increased consumption during the tournament. In the UK alone, on-trade promotions were conducted in more than 5,000 pubs. The majority of Guinness accounts around the world all displayed special Guinness branded Rugby World Cup merchandise and point-of-sale. Many bars and pubs around the world carried an exterior 'Official Guinness Banner' to draw the attention of passers-by and offered three drinks for the price of two during the hour before the kick-off of selected matches thereby encouraging increased traffic to the pubs and encouraging drinkers who would not normally drink Guinness to sample the brand in a great atmosphere.

In the UK, pubs in the vicinity of all Rugby World Cup stadia offered a free 'oversized' foam hat, designed in the shape of a glass of Guinness, for every four pints purchased. This generated huge interest amongst fans and significantly impacted on consumption. In a pub near Twickenham 5,000 pints of Guinness were sold on the day of the England vs. New Zealand match. The added (and planned) benefit was that the fans took the hats into the ground which ensured greater awareness amongst the global television audience.

The UK ran a 'Watch and Win' national on-pack promotion backed by an advertising campaign. The packs of Guinness included a gamecard which featured numbers and consumers needed to watch the television broadcast which featured the winning numbers. The winning numbers equated to various Guinness Rugby World Cup prizes which ranged from vacations to rugby playing nations to inflatable armchairs and at-home supporter kits.

These inflatables were used around the world as well as in the UK and by the end of the tournament, more than 25,000 armchairs and 10,000 pints had been distributed.

PR campaign

Rather than use advertising extensively as a means by which to generate awareness, Guinness chose rather to instigate a comprehensive media PR programme which was rolled out globally and, through close liaison between the agencies in each region, a consistent and clear message was delivered across all markets. In addition to generating awareness through ticket give-aways to radio stations and newspapers, Guinness also worked hard at using PR to create an emotional link between the fans and the brand by creating interesting stories and photo opportunities that would encourage fan response and comment. Examples of such newsworthy angles included the following:

- **The Streaker Prevention Kit**, consisting of a collapsible tube of material which resembled a pint glass of Guinness when placed over a streaker, was issued to all match stewards. A trial of the kit, using a female model, was used for a pre-tournament photo opportunity and generated publicity in the UK, Ireland, Australia and South Africa.

- **The 119½ Second Challenge**, which played on Guinness' advertising prior to the event which claimed that 'It takes 119½ seconds to pour the perfect pint'. The Media PR campaign issued a challenge whereby for any try scored less than 119½ seconds after the start of the game, Guinness donated £10,000 to charity. This is a perfect example of a PR angle which generated interest and comment amongst fans around the world. Through a tie in with the bookmakers Ladbrokes, odds were produced for the players most likely to achieve the feat. Australian Tim Horan did achieve this in Australia's match against Ireland and was pictured after the match, sitting on a Guinness inflatable armchair, with a year's supply of Guinness in crates surrounding him. This highly visual photograph received extensive international coverage. The inflatable armchair was used on a number of other occasions to create additional photo opportunities.

- **Diary Columns** – Realizing that Guinness was unlikely to receive much coverage in match reports, Guinness used diary columns in key local and international media to drive exposure for the brand by featuring humorous stories and statistics regarding Guinness consumption during the event.

- **Trade PR** was also a focus of the PR campaign and ensured that the trade press reported the potential of the Rugby World Cup to the industry so that they would in turn prepare accordingly by increasing stock levels of Guinness during the tournament. The trade press were invited to a function where ex-Springbok captain, François Pienaar, was used as a speaker and the journalists were briefed on the potential of the Rugby World Cup as a spectator event. The trade were further incentivized through opportunities to win matchday tickets and Guinness Rugby World Cup merchandise.

- **The Guinness Media Club** was created for all accredited media covering the event and focused on disseminating information relating to the social, fan-related aspects of the tournament. This allowed Guinness to communicate its brand message directly to key journalists who could influence public perception of the event's success and its sponsors. For a year in advance of the event, more than 600 rugby writers around the world received small items of merchandise and correspondence, culminating with the distribution of more than 4,000 fleeces to all media covering the event itself. In addition four major media parties were held during the tournament and Guinness sponsored the media guide to the event. The media club and the activities associated with it was a significant plank in ensuring that Guinness was pre-eminent amongst the sponsors.

- Guinness produced 10,000 copies of the **Guinness Rugby World Cup Guide** and distributed them to the Guinness Media Club, employees, bars and individual markets for onward distribution and also used some for premiums in Guinness promotions.

Hospitality

Guinness used its hospitality rights to entertain key trade contacts, staff and competition winners across all of its key regions. Throughout the six weeks of the tournament, more than 2,000 international guests were hosted at the Guinness hospitality pavilions.

Internal activation

In addition to match day tickets, the sponsorship was exploited internally through the global staff newsletter, *Guinness Globe*, which featured information on the promotional activities being carried out in the individual markets and contained photographs and stories on the ambassador activity, the broadcast sponsorship and other newsworthy elements of the sponsorship. Competitions to win tickets and merchandise ran in all key markets, and helped to drive a huge level of awareness, interest and focus amongst the critically important internal audience.

Guinness Rugby World Cup ambassadors

Guinness selected a number of ex and current players to serve as Rugby World Cup ambassadors on its behalf during the tournament. These players included François Pienaar, Michael Lynagh, Jonathan Davies and Bob Skinstad. The ambassadors were used at staff and trade events and various campaign launches as well as to help drive the media interest.

Website

In addition to the official Rugby World Cup website, Guinness created its own site focusing on fun and the spectator elements of the event. The website also featured elements of the broadcast sponsorship which could be downloaded and used as screen savers. Research showed that 96 per cent of the visitors to the site considered it to be good fun and the average visit lasted 9 minutes.

Results

Guinness' sponsorship of the Rugby World Cup was a resounding success in terms of everything that the brand set out to achieve.

Firstly, there are a number of examples demonstrating increased consumption in priority markets:

- Great Britain – Sales of Guinness Draught increased by 17 per cent during the Rugby World Cup period and Guinness Draught in cans showed a sales increase of 16 per cent during the same period. The ongoing volume level remained higher than that which had existed prior to the tournament.
- France – Volume sales grew 37 per cent year on year and sale of Guinness Draught increased by 178 per cent against the same period the previous year. The drinker base expanded and research indicated that many drinkers now included Guinness within their drinking repertoire over the long term.
- Australia – Over half a million pints of Guinness were sold across Australia during the Rugby World Cup period which represented a 20 per cent year on year increase. Through the association with what, in Australia, is a sport with a higher and younger profile, the new drinkers recruited to the brand were in exactly the right target range.

- South Africa – The national average throughout increased by 24 per cent between September and November; individual pubs recorded volume increases of 575 per cent, 383 per cent and 324 per cent and sale of Guinness Draught in cans increased 9 per cent year on year.

In terms of achieving top-of-mind awareness and being perceived as the dominant sponsor, Guinness achieved 94 per cent prompted awareness in Great Britain in a post-event study undertaken by Performance Research and further research conducted by TSMS Conductor, ITV's broadcast sponsorship agency, illustrates Guinness' dominance over the other event co-sponsors in terms of the public's awareness of the official sponsors. This dominance amongst consumers was replicated in every major international market in which Guinness undertook activity.

In terms of reinforcing brand essence and injecting energy, promoting newsworthiness and contemporizing the brand, all of Guinness' dominant markets showed positive results.

Table 6.1 Awareness levels of Rugby World Cup sponsors. Reprinted with permission from Diageo

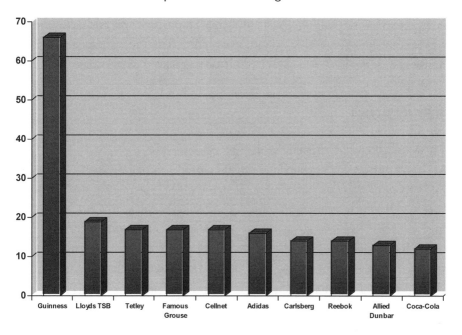

- In Great Britain Guinness claims to have received more than £8 million worth of press coverage and a cumulative circulation of 129 million adults.
- In France PR coverage is said to have reached five million readers.
- In Canada there were an estimated 402,000 impressions on radio listeners, 161,548 impressions on television viewers and 3,339,187 impressions on print media readers with a total circulation of 2.6 million people.
- In South Africa, Bob Skinstad's role as a Guinness Rugby World Cup Ambassador, coupled with the broadcast sponsorship and exploitation plan, helped to significantly rejuvenate the brand image amongst younger drinkers, 18–34 years.

In terms of creating one consistent global brand identity, Guinness achieved this by ensuring that the same Guinness Rugby World Cup logo was used worldwide and through the perimeter signage and broadcast sponsorship deals which it had secured. In addition, the sponsorship leverage 'tool kit' which was distributed to Guinness regions worldwide ensured consistent application of the leverage activities and promotions across all markets.

In terms of motivating and facilitating employees and business partners to exploit the sponsorship, Guinness reported new or increased business across many markets as a direct result of the Rugby World Cup.

KEY INSIGHT

There were four key elements to the Guinness success:

Doing things early: *committing to the event, creating an internal structure and committing budget and strategic planning for the sponsorship was completed nearly 2 years in advance of the event. This allowed markets to focus and develop integrated and powerful tactical plans more than 18 months ahead of the event.*

Brilliant execution: *Having plans in place early meant that markets could focus on exploitation and execution. Roles and responsibilities were clear, and there was total commitment amongst the critical internal audiences. By any measure, execution of plans in markets achieved new levels of excellence.*

Integration and consistency: *The steering group structure meant that plans were fully integrated at both a local and global level. They were not additional to existing market plans and there was therefore focus on the sponsorship as the foundation of plans for the 1998/99 marketing plan. In addition, by conveying a consistent brand message across all its markets globally Guinness was able to maximize the reach of the sponsorship and deliver a clear brand message to its consumers around the world.*

Being true to the brand: *'Only Guinness could do that' was the test for most of the creative exploitation ideas. By executing with a real sense of fun, passion and innovation, the company was able to create a strong emotional link between the brand and its consumers which translated into increased consumption and greater affinity with new drinkers.*

Through the above four approaches, Guinness was able to totally outplay the other event sponsors and achieve its stated objectives.

Leading Thought
Michael Payne, *Marketing Director, International Olympic Committee*

The Olympics has been very different from a marketing standpoint in one key point from all other programmes or properties. Because we have no form of advertising in the venue, or on the athlete, you cannot be lazy in your execution. In an awful lot of other programmes you can always sit back and wait for your name to appear on the television screen and the Chairman and the CEO would be very happy because he saw his name on the box at the weekend. As a result, the other sports sponsorship areas were not immediately forced to look at how to integrate and realize the true potential of that particular property.

At the Olympics you'd end up waiting an awful long time for your name to appear so, from the very beginning of the sponsorship, companies and the Olympic family have been forced to explore exactly how do you use this partnership? How do you integrate it into your ongoing programmes using it as a vehicle for internal staff motivation, for example, when you've got over a million employees?

Advertising, which in many other sports programmes has been the additional extra to the core sponsorship, has become the core function for the Olympic marketing programme and so, over the last 10–15 years, we have been leading the charge in how companies get recall return beyond the traditional sense of billboard advertising.

Ideation – the point of difference

Process can be copied, ideas cannot

Although the passion branding road map will help ensure that a thorough process is followed in the management of passion branding campaigns, it cannot ever be expected to ensure that the campaign itself is liked by consumers or has the necessary impact.

This is where ideation comes into play, the ability of the passion brander to craft a passion branding campaign around a theme or an idea that captures the imagination of the consumer with the resultant positive effect on brand equity and sales.

Creativity applies as much to passion branding as it does to any other form of communication. Just as the 'big idea' is central to the success of a traditional television advertisement, so too is it to the success of a passion branding campaign. This creativity with ideas should be used as the currency of passion branders who at all times need to remain attuned to the environment within which they operate, strategic in their approach whilst opportunistic when appropriate.

Leading Thought
Harlan Stone, *Principal, Velocity Sports & Entertainment*

In today's environment to break through an increasingly commoditized marketing space, creativity is the number 1 element of a successful sponsorship. Not only creativity in finding the right role for a sponsor within a property but creative execution of that role.

For example, Visa has done a terrific job of utilizing the 'everywhere you want to be' creative platform in their Olympic sponsorship. That overall theme and platform has now become a central theme and platform across *all* of their sponsorships. Essentially, Visa will not undertake a sponsorship program unless: a) all marketing departments agree that there is a sufficient creative platform to work off of and b) there is a creative advertising execution that everyone buys into. Not all sponsorships ultimately go 'on air' from a creative perspective. But all sponsorships at least have to pass this litmus test. If a sponsorship is too counterintuitive, and therefore unauthentic, Visa and other 'smart marketers' do not go forward with the sponsorship.

The role of the specialist agency

To deny that the world of passion branding is fraught with pitfalls would be to be out of touch with reality.

I always tell my clients that if they are looking for the easy campaign then they should stick to a traditional media campaign. Passion branding requires hard work and a strong stomach – but with adversity comes opportunity. Get it right and the rewards can be immense. Get it wrong however and you'll be wishing you stuck to the predictable world of 'cut and paste' marketing.

Not only is the industry extremely complicated with few rules or safeguards, but it is also an industry that has no rate card which makes it difficult to navigate and understand, and this is where the services of a reputable specialist agency can be invaluable.

The industry is however not as structured as the traditional above-the-line agency business and it is as well to be aware of the different types of agencies operating in this space.

Agency offerings

Agencies operating in the passion branding space tend to fall into one of three broad categories:

Sales Agencies

These agencies typically represent the property owners, sports federations for example, by whom they have been appointed to raise funding in order to finance the activities of the property owners, such as an event.

They earn their remuneration on a commission basis and may have been required by the property owner to guarantee a certain minimum amount of funding in return for the appointment. As such, the people working for these agencies tend to operate in a high-pressured environment with a focus on the sale rather than on what may be right for the purchaser.

Sales agencies have been around for many years and are by far the most prolific type of agencies operating in the marketplace and range in size from large concerns like IMG and Octagon to one-man operations.

Strategy Consultants

These specialist agencies are quickly growing in number and typically represent the sponsors, i.e. the buyers of rights.

They typically earn their remuneration by way of a consultancy fee paid by the sponsor and are increasingly staffed by marketing professionals who understand the role that sponsorship can play as part of a marketer's tool kit. Their services range from the development of sponsorship strategies and leverage plans through to measurement and evaluation of sponsorships.

They range in size from the larger firms like Octagon, IMG and Momentum to the smaller operations like Redmandarin and Velocity and of course a range of one-man consultancies.

Implementation Agencies

These agencies provide specialist implementation services from media PR to television production and event management.

They typically earn their remuneration by way of implementation fees and are staffed by specialists in the various fields.

Multi-Skilled Agencies

A small number of multi-skilled agencies exist that have combined the above services and offerings to provide the market with a one-stop shop service. Examples include IMG and Octagon, the two largest groups operating in this way with not only the widest spread of capabilities but also the broadest geographic reach.

Working with traditional advertising agencies

Traditional advertising agencies, forced through a changing market to reassess the way in which they function and to a large extent threatened by the growing number of specialist agencies operating in the sponsorship environment, are also starting to offer sponsorship services.

Managing conflicts

One of the ongoing debates within the industry relates to conflicts that potentially may arise where the same agency is providing both sales and consulting services as is the case with IMG and Octagon for example.

The multi-agencies will sell the fact that they offer both services as a benefit rather than something that the client should be concerned with. These benefits include a wider appreciation of market values and properties and a 'first bite' at properties that the agency might represent. They will also claim, quite credibly, that they would not want to damage the relationship between themselves and their clients by offering them a sponsorship property that they represented but that did not have the right strategic fit.

The independent consulting agencies are very quick to highlight this potential conflict and use it as a tactic to win more business away from these multi-skilled agencies.

As with most things in life however it is possible to rationalize any situation and make a case for or against agencies handling both or only one of the two capabilities.

My advice would be to view each case on its merits and before dismissing the multi-agencies to look at the integrity of the agency and specifically the individual people that you are dealing with. There may be instances where it would actually pay you to align yourself with a large multi-agency while there may be instances where the opposite is true. Specialist knowledge or expertise is invaluable in this industry and should always carry a lot of weight in the final analysis as to who you should work with.

Managing global programmes

Coca-Cola have established themselves as one of the leading sponsors of global properties and have in the process developed a highly effective programme that they use to manage their global sponsorships.

World Cup Soccer 2002 proved to be a highly successful sponsorship for Coca-Cola and, apart from being a great example of how a platform can be managed across markets also demonstrates the various levels at which a global platform can be activated and leveraged.

Such was the success of the sponsorship that it is now regarded as the blueprint for the activation of Coca-Cola's other global properties and cross-functional initiatives.

CASE STUDY

Coca-Cola 2002 FIFA World Cup™

Football is one of the most popular sports worldwide, with 250 million registered players globally and 203 national associations affiliated to FIFA and competing for the 32 FIFA World Cup™ slots. The sport is therefore a powerful global communications medium for brands and is an integral part of Coca-Cola's sponsorship portfolio.

In broad terms, the Coca-Cola Company approaches its relationship with football fans in terms of relevance on several levels – globally, pan-regionally, nationally, locally and personally. At each level, the Company and its Operating Divisions assess the opportunities to connect with consumers through football, based on consumer relevance, frequency of events, and other factors. Properties – such as football tournaments, national team sponsorships, player endorsements, grassroots programmes – are chosen selectively by Coca-Cola to deliver against specific fan needs.

Table 6.2 below illustrates the spread of Coca-Cola's football properties. The FIFA World Cup™ is the pinnacle of the game, drawing a cumulative television audience of over 35 billion people and attracting around three million stadium spectators every four years. It is the most valuable sports sponsorship owned by The Coca-Cola Company, given its unique consumer appeal, in terms of reach and local relevance throughout the world, and extensive utilization throughout the Coca-Cola system (more than 100 countries were involved in the World Cup in some way for Korea–Japan 2002).

Table 6.2 Coca-Cola's football properties. Reprinted with permission from The Coca-Cola Company

Football Property	Relevance	Frequency
FIFA World Cup™	Global	Every 4 years
Euro Championships/Africa Cup of Nations	Pan–Regional	1–4 years
National Team/Player Affiliations	National	Yearly
Local Club/Player Affiliations	Local	Weekly
Everyday Player/Youth/Grassroots Activities	Personal	Daily

Teenagers and young adults globally are the largest group playing and following football on a daily basis. However, this audience massively widens during the World Cup. Fans of all ages and both genders from participating countries come together to show their national pride, while football fans in non-participating countries look forward to watching the world's best football teams during this one-month span. The World Cup takes over the daily news for one month, and followers enjoy the best in football as an opportunity to connect and celebrate. The event therefore provides a powerful and unique context for Coca-Cola-inspired refreshment and human connections across a broad target audience as well as significant volume-building opportunities.

Coca-Cola was one of 15 official sponsors to the 2002 FIFA World Cup™ in Korea and Japan, together with other leading brands such as Adidas, MasterCard, McDonalds, Philips and Gillette to name a few. The sponsorship was announced in 1998 and includes several FIFA events until 2006. As a partner sponsor, Coca-Cola was afforded traditional sponsor benefits such as match tickets, presence on-site and exclusivity in the non-alcoholic beverage sector in stadiums as well as some proprietary rights exclusive to Coca-Cola, namely the Flag Bearers national flags, Ball Kids, World Cyber Cup and Official Balls Promotion in 2002.

Coca-Cola's worldwide corporate objectives for the 2002 World Cup were as follows:

- Volume growth for brand Coca-Cola (March/June '02).

- Improved relationship of Coca-Cola with consumers.
- Great on-the-ground experience for consumers and customers at FIFA World Cup.
- Motivate and energize the Coca-Cola system.

Coca-Cola Japan and Korea also added the following objective:

- Build brand equity, generate sustainable profitable volume and increase motivation by utilizing the value of 2002 FIFA World Cup™ Korea/Japan as a 360-degree marketing asset.

These objectives were achieved through a well-managed strategy that could be rolled out with local relevance in each market. The key strategic drivers were as follows:

- The creation of a portfolio of innovative programmes available for all Coca-Cola markets to facilitate activation.
- Full integration of the FIFA World Cup™ into the 2002 Business Plans of Coca-Cola's Top 12 markets (with the exception of the Philippines), based on local business needs.
- Better relations with key international customers; leverage of FIFA World Cup™ by at least three transnational customers.
- Cross-functional initiatives in collaboration with operating divisions; satisfaction from the divisions of the ongoing support provided throughout the project.

Activation of the 2002 FIFA World Cup™ by The Coca-Cola Company was a massive undertaking throughout the Coca-Cola system (corporate, countries/divisions, bottlers). As the most-used marketing platform ever by Coca-Cola, the 2002 event provided a great opportunity to achieve marketing productivity and identify opportunities to further drive efficiencies. The approach to the 2002 World Cup project was also different to previous years, with a clear emphasis on collaboration with operating divisions. Such was the activation of the event that it is now regarded as the blueprint for the activation of Coca-Cola's other global properties and cross-functional initiatives.

Figure 6.2 Cross-functional initiatives in Coca-Cola's 2002 FIFA World Cup™ campaign. Reprinted with permission from The Coca-Cola Company

From January to July 2002, integrated plans across the marketing mix for leveraging the World Cup were executed in more than 100 markets which represented 75 per cent of Coca-Cola worldwide volume. The World Cup was considered a key volume driver for the Coca-Cola brand in April, May and June in nine of the top 10 markets.

Specific World Cup marketing activation activities undertaken by Coca-Cola around the 2002 FIFA World Cup™ were as follows:

Advertising

A combination of globally developed advertising (using three different creative executions – 'Generations,' 'Home Ground Advantage,' and 'Surprise Lesson') and local pieces allowed the Coca-Cola system to capture both the larger-than-life appeal of the World Cup and locally relevant insights through national team support.

In addition, more than 65 spots were produced by individual countries for airing in their local markets.

Figure 6.3 Behind the scenes of Coca-Cola's global television commercial – 'Generations' – featuring Luis Figo, Diego Forlan and Thierry Henry. Reprinted with permission from The Coca-Cola Company

Programmes and Promotions

A wide variety of consumer marketing opportunity blueprints were created centrally by Coca-Cola Marketing Division in collaboration with key markets, external partners – Electronic Arts (EA), Yahoo!, Adidas, Panini – and agencies in order to leverage early the appeal of the event. These programmes allowed Coca-Cola to achieve efficiencies valued in the millions, thanks to pool purchasing and advanced planning. The efforts were complemented by partnership promotions and locally relevant initiatives, where appropriate.

1. Flag Bearers Programme

This involved the selection of 768 teenagers from 19 countries through Coca-Cola promotions and PR activities to carry the flags of the national teams at the opening of each FIFA World Cup™ match.

Figure 6.4 'Surprise Lesson' advertisement. Reprinted with permission from The Coca-Cola Company

2. Ball Kids

768 teenagers from Korea and Japan became part of the on-field competition by serving as 'Ball Kids' along the pitch throughout the tournament. Local activities focused on sports drink promotions with Coca-Cola brands, POWERADE and Aquarius, respectively.

3. Coca-Cola Football Trading Cards/Stickers

By centrally accessing and negotiating player image rights, this popular concept allowed several countries to give away tens of millions of football trading cards and stickers to teenagers around the world. The low premium cost allowed the Coca-Cola system to offer massive collectible giveaways and thus help increase frequency of consumption for brand Coca-Cola.

4. FIFA World Cup™ Trophy events

The world's most recognized trophy toured 15 countries courtesy of Coca-Cola over the course of several months. Local activation not only made this a national happening at each stop, but provided consumers with access to a piece of football glory. Local mechanics ranged from government ties to education contests and non-paid media activation.

Figure 6.5 Coca-Cola flag bearers. Reprinted with permission from The Coca-Cola Company

5. Official 2002 FIFA World Cup™ match balls
Consumers and key constituents around the world were given the chance to receive authentic balls used on the field of play by their football heroes at the FIFA World Cup. A joint activity with FIFA and Adidas, the balls were auctioned on the internet, given away through local promotions (on pack/media), or offered to local constituents, education and internal associates who achieved exceptional results.

6. Merchandise
A global catalogue was developed by Coca-Cola Worldwide Licensing in order to leverage the scale of the event and the Coca-Cola system. More than four million T-shirts, caps, inflatable chairs and other popular items were sold.

7. FIFA World Cup™ ticket giveaway promotions
The vast majority of Coca-Cola's World Cup ticket allotment was used throughout the Coca-Cola network in consumer promotions, leveraging the appeal of attending the largest football spectacle.

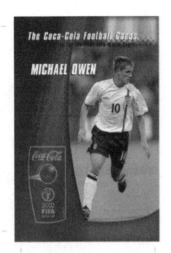

Figure 6.6 Football trading cards. Reprinted with permission from The Coca-Cola Company

Figure 6.7 Trophy Tour – Vietnam. Reprinted with permission from The Coca-Cola Company

Figure 6.8 Coca-Cola World Cup Trophy Tour event. Reprinted with permission from The Coca-Cola Company

Online Marketing

Coca-Cola launched various breakthrough online programmes aimed specifically at its teenager target audience. These programmes included the following:

1. Coca-Cola World Cyber Cup

Through a marketing partnership with Electronic Arts, 11 countries from around the world participated in a breakthrough, pre-match 'cyber competition.' Eleven youths, selected through local promotions online and offline, competed in World Cup video games on the giant screens of the World Cup stadia. This event was leveraged not only in each of the 11 countries, but through globally developed stories for non-paid media and PR.

Figure 6.9 Ticket give-away promotions – Korea. Reprinted with permission from The Coca-Cola Company

2. Coca-Cola Pooling Game

Conducted in association with Yahoo!, this popular interactive fantasy game allowed consumers around the world to guess the scores and outcomes of FIFA World Cup matches for local activation prizes. The internet-based game was developed in nine languages and activated with 24 countries.

Public relations

The use of public relations (PR) enhanced the impact of consumer promotions by delivering core messages to media around the world and by leveraging the Coca-Cola company's proprietary programmes to ensure high impact and visibility.

1. Coca-Cola Go! Stadium Art Programme

Twenty-five of the 32 participating FIFA World Cup countries leveraged the opportunity to customize the traditional billboards on the FIFA World

Figure 6.10 The Coca-Cola Cyber Cup. Reprinted with permission from The Coca-Cola Company

Cup pitch and turn them into a contour bottle 'canvas' to reflect their national team support. Local activities for coming up with the final billboard designs included trade promotions, art contests, and government and education initiatives. The programme proved to be highly successful (there were 18,000 entries in China!). The GO! programme provided significant additional value to a static awareness piece and was the programme that generated the most interest and coverage from the media.

2. PR tool kit and media website
Coca-Cola developed a comprehensive PR field tool kit to cover all marketing mix activities and also produced a website for the media (www.football.cocacola.com). The website included top-line stories about Coca-Cola World Cup programmes as well as further information about the company's involvement with the sport around the world.

Hospitality

An extensive hospitality programme enabled key company and bottler decision-makers to strengthen relationships with their constituents (customers, governments, strategic partners etc.).

Figure 6.11 Internal staff motivation programme. Reprinted with permission from The Coca-Cola Company

Internal Motivation

A tool kit containing key facts about the World Cup, Coca-Cola's activation efforts around the world, and 'thought starters' to leverage the event with Coca-Cola employees was developed and rolled out to human resources managers in all regions. Activities included replicating the Coca-Cola GO! Stadium Art Programme as an internal contest, viewing parties around match broadcasts, an internal bracket game and merchandise giveaways.

Activities specific to the host countries

Korea and Japan not only leveraged FIFA World Cup™ excitement in their respective countries through several marketing activities during the 12 months leading up the event (including most of the programmes developed centrally), but also integrated the execution of the company's value-in-kind obligations – such as the supply of beverages to the football and media families and venue consumption – into their operation goals. This was achieved through active collaboration with their respective bottlers at all levels, as well as close cooperation with local authorities in the 10 venue cities in each country. This greatly reinforces the ability of the Coca-Cola systems to take advantage of future opportunities in those markets.

Joint leverage activities with other partner sponsors

In addition to the activation programmes which Coca-Cola carried out on its own to leverage its association with the event, Coca-Cola also initiated a number of highly successful joint programmes with other FIFA World Cup sponsors which further maximized the benefits achieved through the sponsorship.

1. FIFA World Cup™ Video Game & Coca-Cola World Cyber Cup
(In association with Electronic Arts partnership)
Coca-Cola was a partner with Electronic Arts Sports (EA Sports), the world's leading interactive entertainment software company, to offer a special-edition 'pre-release' version of EA Sports' official *FIFA World Cup™ Video Game* for 2002. Beginning in March 2002, the pre-release of the game was made available to consumers through Coca-Cola in more than 30 participating countries. Depending on demand, the game – which featured significant Coca-Cola brand presence and a link to *coca-cola.com* – was available in as many as eight languages. The CD-ROM video game is compatible with personal computer platforms.

The dynamic video game, The Coca-Cola Cyber World Cup, was another joint initiative between Coca-Cola and EA. This competition was open to any country, not only those participating in the FIFA World Cup event.

2. The Coca-Cola 2002 FIFA World Cup™ Game
(In association with Yahoo!® Sports)
This was a fun, and highly interactive, global game which allowed people around the world to share their predictions for 2002 FIFA World Cup matches.

Through *The Coca-Cola 2002 FIFA World Cup™ Game* – created in association with, and hosted by, Yahoo!® Sports – consumers shared their

Figure 6.12 GO! Stadium Art Programme. Reprinted with permission from The Coca-Cola Company

forecasts and competed with other fans at home and in other countries by logging on to either *www.coca-cola.com*, a country-specific Coca-Cola website, or other partner websites. The web-based programme allowed people around the world to play, interact and have fun together, while at the same time enabling local Coca-Cola offices to activate this tool according to their strategies. The game was developed in nine languages – English, Spanish, French, German, Italian, Portuguese, Japanese, Korean and Simplified Chinese.

Once the FIFA World Cup™ began, online players received points for correctly predicting a match's winning team and final score. Players with the most points by country at the conclusion of the tournament were announced game champions. Game sites featured a link to the online Coca-Cola/FIFA world rankings and other football sites, such as Yahoo!® Sports football coverage, in order to assist participants with current statistics. Coca-Cola sent participants daily notifications via e-mail and participants were able to match their picks against other contestants in their respective countries, or worldwide, or against a select group of friends, or as one nation against another.

3. Official 2002 FIFA World Cup™ Match Balls
(In association with Adidas and FIFA)
As part of its FIFA World Cup™ sponsorship, Coca-Cola had the right to run promotions using Adidas® footballs from each 2002 FIFA World Cup™ match. Following each game, one match ball was awarded to Coca-Cola

representatives from each of the two competing countries to be used in consumer programmes and promotions before, during or after the tournament.

Results

The 2002 FIFA World Cup™ effectively created a step change in the way it demonstrated how a powerful passion branding platform can help to build the Coca-Cola business, creating sustainable legacies for the Coca-Cola system.

Through leveraging the global appeal of the World Cup, The Coca-Cola Company solidified its relations with consumers around the world because it provided a unique World Cup experience on the ground in all parts of the world. Coca-Cola was also able to maximize volume increases during the event and lay the groundwork for sustainable growth, particularly in Korea and Japan. Coca-Cola's event activation improved the company's relationship with major international customers, as well as with staff, in that it helped to re-energize the Coca-Cola system and create excitement among employees thus reinforcing their pride to work in The Coca-Cola Company system. The strong and exciting public relations efforts also played a major role in generating positive, targeted consumer awareness and attitudes about Coca-Cola brands and their relevant and unique connection with the FIFA World Cup™.

Specific results of Coca-Cola's activation of the World Cup are as follows:

1. Relationship with consumers

- Many key markets showed growth for brand Coca-Cola across most of the key brand metrics such as consumption levels, awareness, favourite brand and purchase intent.
- Goals varied by country and were not always focused on brand metrics. Local measurement criteria were set up in these cases to gauge the success of the sponsorship in terms of local objectives.

2. International customer relations

- Successful customer activation showed improved relationships and solid growth in the promotional period and created a sustainable activation platform for everyday football.

3. On-site consumer and customer experiences
- Successful event management operation showed a record incidence in venues compared to World Cup '98.
- High satisfaction from consumers and guests regarding the on-the-ground experience.

4. Energizing the System
- Integrated efforts with PR created high system awareness and education on the World Cup through external affairs updates and centralized media stories.
- Internal motivation programme in the US delivered a high level of interest and response at Coca-Cola's Atlanta Headquarters.

5. Additional selected business results
Corporate
- The World Cup was used as a true marketing platform in most of Coca-Cola's top 15 markets over a longer time frame than in the past (starting in March/April in most divisions).
- Marketing alliances and partnerships with football-relevant third parties such as EA, Adidas and Panini allowed for synergies and enhanced relationships and maximized the benefits that could be derived from sponsoring the event.
- New and innovative programmes were successfully implemented (e.g. Stadium Art and Cyber Cup) and will be considered for other global events sponsored by Coca-Cola such as Rugby World Cup, Euro 2004.
- The FIFA World Cup™ was successfully leveraged by some key transnational customers such as Carrefour, 7-Eleven and Blockbuster).

Coca-Cola (Japan) Company Ltd.
- For the Coca-Cola system in Japan, this was the first time that Coca-Cola (Japan) Company Ltd and its 15 bottlers had worked together for one marketing asset to integrate throughout Japan.
- Coca-Cola was able to minimize incremental budget and labour using 1/3 of the Nagano Games budget and 3/4 of the size of the project team.

Coca-Cola (Korea) Company Ltd.

- Coca-Cola achieved all-time record high sales volumes in Korea in June.
- The FIFA World Cup™ brought the excitement and pride to the employees of the Coca-Cola system in Korea.
- The successful operation of joint project groups together with the Coca-Cola Korea Bottling Company was the first time ever that they had worked together as one team reaching for the same goals.
- The activation in Japan and Korea set a new standard for how host countries should take advantage of Coca-Cola's global properties.

Coca-Cola identified many key learnings from the 2002 FIFA World Cup™ that will be taken into account in future World Cup events and on other global properties that the company supports. Firstly, while the World Cup is a powerful equity driver for brand Coca-Cola when properly activated and leveraged using innovative marketing and PR programmes, further effectiveness and integration, particularly in communication, must always be measured and attained. Coca-Cola must also continually strive for increased efficiencies especially considering the massive investments at stake. Secondly, the World Cup demonstrated that global properties represent a key business opportunity with Coca-Cola's transnational customers, such as 7-Eleven and Blockbuster, and these should be better leveraged to achieve greater results. Thirdly, host country and hospitality support can achieve additional success by expanding the scope of activities undertaken. Finally, events of the stature of the World Cup can play a highly effective role in energizing all staff within the Coca-Cola system and generating cross functional initiatives between the company's corporate functions, operating divisions and customer groups and the potential of these should be further capitalized upon.

KEY INSIGHT

The success of Coca-Cola's activation of the 2002 FIFA World Cup™ can largely be attributed to the way in which the global platform was made relevant to football fans and Coca-Cola consumers around the world through locally relevant executions of innovative leverage programmes aimed at solidifying relations with fans. By establishing a core team, supported by an ongoing network that had access to easy-to-use tools, and who were kept informed through regular communications, Coca-Cola was able to manage the implementation of the project and ensure that integration, consistency and effective results were achieved in all markets.

Managing multi-sponsor programmes

As the costs associated with large passion platforms escalate, a feature that is becoming increasingly more prevalent is that of multi-sponsor programmes. In such instances, a number of sponsors will be offered the opportunity to share their association with a passion platform with a number of other non-competing sponsors.

While this approach is now well established worldwide it pays to understand some of the risks and benefits associated with these types of programmes.

Benefits
- Rights fees shared between sponsors allowing for a greater investment in leverage around the sponsorship.
- Co-promotions and business opportunities with other co-sponsors.
- Value transfer between co-sponsors.

Risks
- Sponsor clutter, i.e. too many sponsors making it difficult to be noticed.
- Other co-sponsors doing a better leverage job than you and stealing the limelight.
- Poor delivery of rights by platform owners. It is easier to service one sponsor than six!
- Category creep, i.e. where a co-sponsor, who operates the same (or similar) type of business as you, takes up sponsorship rights in a

different category from yours. Their participation may indirectly dilute your efforts to influence consumers in your selected category.[1]

Exit strategy management

Passion branding requires a long-term commitment between a sponsoring brand and a platform owner if it is to achieve its full potential.

As such, when embarking upon a new passion branding campaign, it pays to consider in advance of entering into the relationship with the platform owner what the total investment required over this period might be and put in place the checks and balances to allow you to appropriately manage this relationship.

An exit may come about as a result of any number of reasons including an increase in rights fees or leverage costs, poor delivery by the platform itself or a change in business focus. In each instance, consideration should ideally be given at contract stage as how best to deal with any eventuality so as to avoid any potential conflicts with the platform owner in the future.

Careful consideration therefore needs to be taken when a decision is taken to exit from a passion branding relationship, for whatever reason. A detailed exit strategy should be developed that addresses each set of stakeholders and sets out how the exit will be managed and communicated with them.

Passion branding is not only a long-term commitment to the platform owner but also more importantly with the platform's passionate fans. As much as the loyalty towards a sponsoring brand can be nurtured amongst passionate fans through a successful passion branding campaign, so too can it be destroyed by a sponsoring brand's decision to no longer support the passion platform concerned.

---

[1]   A good example is the following: In the 2003 Cricket World Cup SAA was the Official Global Airline partner for the event while Sahara was the Indian team's sponsor. Sahara is a big Indian conglomerate that operates in a range of categories including a regional airline in India. As a result of SAA's sponsorship of the Cricket World Cup, the Indian team were precluded from carrying Sahara's branding on their shirts because SAA objected in an effort to protect their rights and category creep from Sahara.

There is no template that I can provide you with that will help you through this 'exit' process other than to suggest that the use of common sense and a degree of compassion will probably get you through what will in all likelihood be an uneasy experience. Open and honest communication with fans will go a long way to maintaining the trusting relationship that you will have hopefully nurtured with them over the years.

Contract management

Just as the case with any relationship with a third party, it is wise to put your agreement in writing in the form of a legal contract for the purposes of regulating the basis of the relationship between you and the third party as well as setting out performance expectations on both sides.

Given the complexities of the passion branding environment, I would strongly urge that a suitably experienced lawyer who understands the ins and outs of the industry, and the potential pitfalls, should draft such agreements.

This is particularly important in the area of broadcast rights which can be very complex in nature with issues such as territory (e.g. worldwide vs. limited geographic area) and the nature of the rights (e.g. free-to-air vs. satellite) potentially having a major implication on what it is that you are actually buying.

Managing effective sponsorship programmes

Sponsorships do not always enjoy a high priority in the communications mix. Where this is the case, they tend not to command the interest of the senior marketing people in the business, often being relegated to the status of 'second class citizen'. As we have seen throughout this text, sponsorship provides a platform off which a wide range of business objectives can be achieved. In practice however, rights secured by sponsors are rarely used across the full spectrum of opportunity.

This is a poor reflection on the way in which the majority of sponsorships are managed. There are still far too many sponsorship managers who understand the sport their brands are associated with better than they do the basics of integrated marketing communications.

Passion branding management needs to be treated with respect for it is probably one of the most complex areas within communication. From understanding and dealing with brands and consumers one minute, to negotiating complex rights and broadcast deals the next, the new passion brander needs to be a multi-talented commercially savvy individual.

Responsible marketing directors should also think twice before delegating the responsibility for managing and leveraging their passion branding campaigns to junior staff as to do so will potentially put them at risk of wasted opportunity and even more importantly wasted budgets. On-the-job learning and coaching from a good sponsorship consultant are the quickest way to get to grips with this complex, and at times confusing, discipline.

Leading Thought
Sean O'Neill, *Brand & Communication Director, Diageo*

We are a company with an unparalleled record of delivering fantastic consumer advertising which has helped us deliver impressive brand growth. Unfortunately, where sponsorship is concerned, this track record has meant that as a business we have looked more to advertising as a first response to a given consumer issue rather than any other disciplines, including sponsorship.

As a result, our advertising credentials are absolutely sensational and our general marketing capability is sensational but we have yet to raise the bar in areas like sponsorship. I am currently leading a project which will address this as part of our overall approach to marketing within the business.

I firmly believe that sponsorship needs to be absolutely rooted in what the brand need is, what is relevant and important to the consumer and compatible with the work underway in our markets. The reality is that until we have completed our strategic sponsorship work, we will not have the level of sophistication which enables us to achieve this.

Leading Thought
Michael Brockbank, *Vice President Brand Communications,*
Unilever

Our brands are big. We invest about $4 billion communicating with our brands' consumers each year and relatively little of this is currently assigned to sponsorship. In the USA for instance, sponsorship accounted for only 4 per cent of our marketing expenditure in 2001. We believe there is a clear opportunity to accelerate our brands' growth using sponsorship more widely.

We started this process with a major quantitative research survey amongst over 400 Unilever brand marketers to get a sense of their understanding and use of sponsorship to date. Between 2000–2002, 46 of our markets have used sponsorship, and of those, 73 per cent thought that sponsorship had been quite, or very, effective and 75 per cent thought sponsorship effectively strengthened our brand values. 44 per cent felt that our investment in sponsorship should increase a little or increase a lot. 'There are potentially creative ways to be involved with sponsorship that we have not even begun to explore in Unilever,' said one respondent.

What has happened over the last few years is that there has been a huge explosion of new opportunities in marketing. There is however also a lack of skills and experience levels to handle these new opportunities as well as an understandable reluctance to move into new areas where they do not have the comfort of historical measures.

In response to this, and in recognition of the increasing role that sponsorship is going to play at Unilever in the future, we have developed a way that Unilever thinks about sponsorship which is expressed in a workshop and in a manual and will be on our website. We will be taking our global brand teams and key companies through a workshop to help them a) understand better how sponsorship could help their brand and; b) help them to use sponsorship more effectively as a tool when they do so.

7

Measurement – accountability and return on investment

One of the biggest challenges facing passion branding is the extent to which it can be measured. The discipline's biggest critics are often the traditional above-the-line agencies as the language that they use, and the measurement principles that they apply, seem to have little in common with much from the world of passion branding.

Passion branding is as much about the 'soft' or intangible benefits as it is about the 'hard' or tangible benefits. Despite the immense value of these soft benefits, they are often discounted by those wanting to discredit passion branding and in the process they are given little recognition.

Measurement of the benefits of passion branding will never be a science. This, coupled with the fact that each passion branding campaign will have its very own specific objectives, means that there will never be any one measurement tool that can be applied to all passion branding campaigns.

What is important rather is that there should be a continual debate around the issue of measurement of passion branding. There needs to be a consistency in application of whatever measurement model is being used to allow for benchmarking of results from one period to the next together with a commitment to measure and evaluate all passion branding activities on an ongoing basis.

A commitment to measurement also requires that sufficient budget is set aside to ensure that adequate measurement and evaluation of results can actually take place.

What is also required is the recognition that the discipline of passion branding needs to become accountable if the huge amounts of money being invested in the discipline are to be continued. Competition for resources within the corporate world is ever increasing and those marketing or communication initiatives that are able to demonstrate a meaningful return on investment in a logical and robust manner will win the day. Those that do not will be relegated to the trash heap never to see the light of day.

Measurement drives behaviour and can therefore become a strong ally of any brand wanting to focus its efforts in a particular direction. In sponsorship contracts with passion property owners there is a strong case for including certain measurement criteria, those that they can directly influence, with the added incentive that if certain objectives are measured and met, then a bonus will be paid.

The same can apply to service contracts entered into with specialist passion branding agencies in order that they can be incentivized to focus on delivering against certain objectives. At Octagon in South Africa we use the latter approach on a number of clients. Our performance against certain pre-determined objectives is evaluated by an independent third party acceptable to both ourselves and our clients on the understanding that the decision of this third party is final. Our clients are happy to pay us the bonus if we achieve their objectives and we are happy to use the scheme to focus our client service teams' efforts on what is really important to the client.

Effect vs. output

We've all seen examples of sponsorships where the only measure of success is the output generated by the sponsorship with little, if any, cognisance given to whether that output is relevant. The wad of press cuttings dropped on the table by the over-zealous PR consultant, half of which did not convey the appropriate message and the other half from irrelevant media, is something you have probably experienced first hand.

Do not subject yourself to this outdated measurement philosophy – output as a focus is dead in the passion economy. What counts now is effect; the effect of the passion branding campaign on whatever it is that you are trying to influence through passion branding, be it brand equity or sales or some other specific and measurable objective.

This simple change in focus, from output to effect, has major implications for the accountability of passion branding – well, for those practitioners willing to subscribe to this new approach – and provides a strong basis upon which passion branding campaigns can be managed and held accountable.

Leading Thought
Sally Hancock, *Chief Executive, Redmandarin*

We believe that there are two relative measures in sponsorships – one is the measure of output and the other is the measure of outcome.

The measure of output is basically, 'How many people were watching? How many were in the stadium? How many people read it in the newspapers? How many minutes were broadcast?' and so on which is fine but doesn't tell you whether there was any kind of change in consumer behaviour as a result of that output. The trouble is that most rights holders sell everything they sell on the basis of measures of output.

We do need to have an understanding of the reach of a sponsorship and the exposure of it and a number of opportunities to see the sponsor. What is more relevant however is a measure of outcome and actually what people think and do as a result of seeing it – did it motivate them to consider buying your product more often?

We believe very strongly in this idea of output and outcome and there are a number of different ways of getting to the outcome of a sponsorship. Of course it all depends on objectives, as we all know. But on the one hand it's the question of understanding the effect of the sponsorship on the perception of the sponsoring brand if that was an objective, or, even more concretely, how many extra products were sold as a direct result of this sponsorship?

What I am very careful about saying is that it is very difficult to isolate the effect of sponsorship for most brands when there is a lot of other promotional activity at the same time. Unless you can directly attribute sales to the fact that you sold them outside the football grounds on that particular day or you had a promotion that was directly linked to your sponsorship of that football team, just by having perimeter boards at an event is not going to have a direct effect on your sales downstream that you can isolate and I wouldn't believe anyone that told me that you could.

Leading Thought
Michael Brockbank, *Vice President Brand Communication, Unilever*

Firstly we found that sponsorship is in many ways the same as other communication activities. In terms of objectives, we have to apply the same 'abc criteria'. Our programme has to reach the consumers and get their attention. The brand has to be clearly communicated. Communication has not only to be clear, but also relevant.

The output of the activity may be a good measure of the quality of its implementation: how many people saw it, for how long? But what really matters is the outcome of the communication: how it affected the behaviour of the brand's consumers. So it's a pity that when sponsorship agencies and rights owners talk to our marketers, so many of them talk almost exclusively about outputs, and leave us to concern ourselves with the outcome.

Secondly we found a host of ways in which sponsorship is different to other communication activities. We make sure our teams are aware of these differences, and we give them clear guidance on how to address them.

Quantitative and qualitative measures

There are a range of quantitative measures that can be used when measuring passion branding effectiveness.

'Free' media coverage

The best known of these is probably the advertising equivalent value of 'free' media generated around a passion branding campaign. Paul Vaughan, a former colleague at Octagon and now Commercial Manager for the RFU, once described the values arrived at through these types of measurement as 'spurious'. I was not familiar with the word at the time so I looked it up and now understand it to mean any of 'fake', 'false', 'bogus', 'counterfeit', 'deceptive', 'deceitful', 'phoney' or 'fictitious'. I think that is a pretty good description.

The value to a brand of editorial type media coverage is not in question, nor the wonderful role that passion branding can play in providing a platform off which 'free' media can be leveraged for the benefit of a sponsoring brand. What is in question however is the manner in which this 'free' media is measured.

For example, here is how free media might be measured:

Determine the number of column centimetres of coverage received by the sponsored activity and apply the following multiples:

– Colour pictures: valued at 5 times advertising rate card.
– Black and white pictures: valued at 3 times advertising rate card.
– Editorial: valued at 2 times advertising rate card.

This then provides a dollar value for the coverage received. A similar methodology is applied to electronic media like television and radio. A two-column article including a colour picture that mentioned the sponsor's name once would therefore be valued at many multiples of what it would cost to place a print advertisement dedicated in full to the brand. Spurious!

This measurement philosophy is grounded in the old output approach to sponsorships and makes no consideration for the efficacy of the coverage received – things like the relevance of the media in which the coverage appeared; the extent to which the sponsor's key messages have been conveyed in the editorial; the extent to which sponsor identification by way of branding appears in any pictures or editorial; the strength of association between the passion platform and the sponsoring brand and, as a result, the effect of the coverage on readers.

It would seem far more logical and appropriate that the value of 'free' media coverage to a sponsoring brand be measured on the basis that, firstly all irrelevant media coverage is stripped out and, secondly, a premium rate only applied to coverage that either highlighted a key message or theme of the sponsoring brand or made a very strong association between the passion platform and the sponsoring brand.

Leading Thought

David Butler, *Head of Laureus Sport For Good Foundation and Manager of Laureus World Sports Academy*

Sponsorship is multi-dimensional so only a multi-dimensional evaluation system is of any use. I used to be a PR director in sponsorship where media generated was of a prime importance – because we were still being driven by the advertisers' model. We were playing on someone else's playing field! Sponsorship is not only about media awareness – media awareness where? Targeted to whom? Saying what? Relating how to sale? We were in a culture where the big number at the end had to rise every year by 20 per cent. Then go and advertise! Sponsorship is a tailor-made suit and therefore cannot be judged alone on the number of admiring glances. Does it fit? What is it saying about the wearer? Does it wear well – is it sustainable? Is it suited to the climate? Does the colour match? Who is giving the admiring glances? Sometimes there is no return on investment – neither financially nor in media inches. The first question is why are you sponsoring? What is trying to be achieved? Is it positive association or is it sales led? The measurement tool needs to reflect all these individual needs so it will always be different – that is a strength of the sponsorship tool!

Changes in awareness

If heightened awareness is an objective on a passion branding campaign, then tracking consumer awareness of the passion branding campaign on an ongoing basis, pre- and post-campaign, can be used to assess changes in awareness levels.

These studies usually call for prompted and unprompted awareness and one would expect to find a higher awareness level in response to the prompted as opposed to the unprompted question.

Awareness on its own can be a dangerous indicator of success. There are many examples where a campaign has delivered a high awareness level while further investigation reveals that very little is understood by consumers as to the product offering or brand image. One example was Green Flag's high-profile sponsorship of the English soccer team which delivered high awareness scores for the Green Flag brand but low scores for what it was that Green Flag actually did (for those of you that still don't know, they are a breakdown service in the UK and very similar to the AA).

I know sponsors who live and die by the results of the next awareness tracking survey. I do not believe however that this, in and of itself, is sufficient to determine if a campaign is achieving its objectives or not.

Leading Thought
Michael Payne, *Marketing Director, International Olympic Committee*

The whole debate on recall totally misses the point. It's like turning around and saying who advertised on television last night? Whether you can recall or not who was advertising on television, it doesn't bring into question whether the campaign was necessarily working or not.

What you've rather got to do is to measure the effectiveness of the sponsorship in taking the marketing decision into the moment of purchase and to measure what the factors are that are pushing the consumer to decide 'I want to purchase A or B' through to what are the factors that are creating the general sub-conscious perspective that the consumer has of company A or B – and to that extent the sports world plays a critical role in helping to define a company's image.

To start with the company has to have a clear understanding and vision of why it is doing the sponsorship. An awful lot of people weighed in feet first, without a clear vision or plan of what it is they want to get out of this. So, first make sure that you develop the activation review programmes according to your objectives. Second, be aware that, as with any form of marketing, it's not always easy to isolate exactly what is causing that particular return versus everything else that is going on because you've got different programme campaigns happening all the time.

Sales

This can be both the simplest and most difficult thing to measure.

It works best when a very short-term localized promotion has been linked to a passion branding campaign and can be compared to sales in other regions where no such promotions took place. Likewise, where a passion platform specific database has been used to run a promotion (e.g. a list of registered club members at a football club) the measurement is relatively easy. It is also relatively easy to measure where a new business channel may have been opened up as a direct result of a passion branding linked initiative.

While most other categories of measurement can be commissioned and provided by the passion platform owners, the sales piece of the measurement puzzle can really only be undertaken by the sponsoring brand as the property owner has little, if any, direct involvement in the sales process of its sponsors.

Leading Thought
Harlan Stone, *Principal, Velocity Sports & Entertainment*

Sponsorship can drive trackable sales results better than most forms of marketing – and can do it in an environment where it drives an emotional connection at the same time. Although sponsor organizations have under utilized CRM, a properly handled sponsorship program should generate significant data about attendees including post event sales activity <u>and</u> qualitative results concerning attendee's attitudes toward the sponsorship program.

For example, BMW has a program called the 'ultimate test drive'. It's a program that is elegant in its simplicity. Essentially BMW direct mails owners of competitor products and invites them to the ultimate test drive (a comparison drive i.e. drive the Mercedes through a variety of 'test' zones and then drive the BMW's through the same zones.) Immediately following this exciting experience consumers are given an incentive to come to the show room and test drive and are then tracked over the next 1, 3, 6 and 12 month periods to see the results. Not only is there a terrific 'experiential' event but there's firm tracking results to go along.

Leading Thought
Lawrence Flanagan, *Executive Vice President and Chief Marketing Officer for Global Marketing, MasterCard International*

We measure two things. We measure awareness levels in the market and we use a marketing mix model where we track actual lift in GDV, (Gross Dollar Volume) the actual spend on MasterCard throughout the year.

It's a fairly sophisticated arithmetic model that the Hudson River Group have developed for us and that we've been using for about 5 years now and from which we can actually see, against specific programmes, if we did see a lift in business or not.

When we do these big integrated sponsorship-led programmes we actually do see a lift in our business and a higher return versus even our core basic brand message communication.

Quality is as important, if not more important, than quantity

It is not only quantitative measures that are important. In fact, many of passion branding's strongest attributes are qualitative in nature, particularly those that relate to brand building and consumer attitudes. These are best measured through the brand tracking studies that most brands subscribe to.

Detractors of passion branding will often argue that it is not possible to determine what brand benefits have arisen as a direct result of a passion branding campaign. Octagon and research house Millwood Brown have however developed a response to this criticism in the form of *The Sponsorship Effect*, a model which highlights the difference in response from consumers exposed to the sponsorship against those not exposed to the sponsorship. Any difference in response is attributed to the sponsorships.

CASE STUDY

Samsung beach volleyball sponsorship in Brazil: measuring the sponsorship effect

Samsung appointed Millward Brown to carry out research on its sponsorship of beach volleyball in Brazil in order to:

- Isolate the genuine effects of the sponsorship.
- Identify strengths and weakness of the programme.
- Verify the event performance in terms of attendees and their reaction, likes and dislikes to the event.
- Monitor the changes in the consumer brand relationship as a result of the sponsorship in terms of improved brand awareness, image, consideration and favourability of the brand.

In broad terms the research needed to identify if the sponsorship actively contributed towards the growth of the brand, and if so, by how much and whether it was achieved in a cost effective manner, with the end result being that Samsung would be left with actionable data for both tactical and strategic planning in the next sponsorship cycle.

Research was conducted over a two-week period after the event in Greater Florianopolis using telephone interviews with 300 men and women, 150 of whom were exposed to the Samsung sponsorship and 150 of whom were not.

The results are captured below in the various graphs and tables:

1. The brand in its marketplace

Table 7.1 Spontaneous Brand Awareness – Mobile Phones. Reprinted with permission from Samsung

Brands	Top of Mind		Total Mentions	
	Exposed %	Not Exposed %	Exposed %	Not Exposed %
Nokia	25	27	63	54
Samsung	**22**	**7**	**55**	**23**
Ericsson	15	15	44	39
Motorola	15	14	49	37
Tim	6	11	8	16
Gradiente	5	5	29	27
Global	3	5	13	15
Teem	3	5	3	6
LG	3	4	25	19
Sony	–	–	1	2
Panasonic	–	–	1	0
Qualcomm	–	–	0	1
	150	150	150	150

Table 7.2 Spontaneous Brand Awareness – Monitors. Reprinted with permission from Samsung

Brands	Top of Mind		Total Mentions	
	Exposed %	Not Exposed %	Exposed %	Not Exposed %
LG	23	19	39	29
Samsung	33	23	52	41
IBM	4	5	7	8
Compaq	3	2	5	4
Philips	1	3	11	9
HP	1	0	3	0
Itautec	1	1	3	2
Panasonic	1	1	1	2
Semp Toshiba	1	0	3	1
Sony	–	–	5	1
TCE	–	–	1	0
	150	150	150	150

Table 7.3 Brand Health Prompted – Mobile Phones. Reprinted with permission from Samsung

Brands	Heard of		Have Today		Would Consider on Next Purchase		Favourite	
	Exposed %	Not Exposed %	Exposed %	Not Exposed %	Exposed %	Not Exposed %	Exposed %	Not Exposed %
Nokia	97	96	31	25	49	45	29	29
Motorola	96	97	19	10	29	22	13	11
Samsung	93	83	9	8	41	15	21	9
Gradiente	93	96	13	9	17	13	5	5
Ericsson	92	95	25	27	17	16	7	9
LG	65	69	8	5	12	7	2	2
Sony	55	66	0	1	7	4	1	1
Qualcomm	12	11	0	1	1	2	0	1
Global	2	1	1	1	1	0	1	0
Tim	1	1	1	1	2	1	2	1
Teem	1	1	1	1	0	0	0	0
	150	150	150	150	150	150	150	150

Table 7.4 Brand Health Prompted – Monitors. Reprinted with permission from Samsung

Brands	Heard of		Have Today		Would Consider on Next Purchase		Favourite	
	Exposed %	Not Exposed %	Exposed %	Not Exposed %	Exposed %	Not Exposed %	Exposed %	Not Exposed %
Samsung	**89**	**93**	**20**	**21**	**63**	**32**	**33**	**17**
LG	83	83	29	19	37	32	17	17
Philips	68	74	8	5	28	25	9	11
TCE	32	40	2	1	5	4	1	0
HP	1	0	1	0	–	–	–	–
IBM	1	1	1	1	–	–	–	–
Itautetc	1	0	1	0	–	–	–	–
Semp Toshiba	1	0	1	0	0	1	1	0
Compaq	1	1	1	1	1	1	1	0
Panasonic	–	–	–	–	1	0	–	–
Sony	–	–	–	–	0	1	0	1
	150	150	150	150	150	150	150	150

Table 7.5 Reasons for Preference – Monitors. Reprinted with permission from Samsung

	Total %	Exposed %	Not Exposed %
It doesn't show any problem/faults Repairing/Not easily broken/Never needed assistance	36	30	46
Is a good brand/Great brand/Good quality	25	24	27
Clear images/Better image definition/better image visualisation (focus)	22	20	27
Beautiful Design/Modern/Thin	21	26	12
Habit/Used to the brand/Used it for a long time	20	18	23
Monitor's Characteristics/Flat screen/Bigger screen/Transparent	13	14	12
Well known brand	12	14	8
Good colour definition/Bright colours	11	8	15
Easy to use/Easy to connect to the Internet/ Easy to settle	9	8	12
Well spoken language	8	6	12
Advanced technology/better technology	8	10	4
Product Options/Lots of options	7	10	0
Long lasting	5	2	12
Has more resources/functions/All that I need (general)	5	2	12
	(76)	(50)	(26)

Table 7.6 Reasons for Preference – Mobile Phones. Reprinted with permission from Samsung

	Total %	Exposed %	Not Exposed %
Small/Small Format/Compact/Light (fits anywhere)	41	44	36
Beautiful Design/Modern/Thin	41	53	14
It doesn't show any problem/Faults/ Repairing/Not easily broken/ Never needed assistance	15	6	36
Model Options/Lots of sizes/Lots of colours	15	19	7
You can access the Internet/e-mail WAP	15	9	29
Has more resources/Functions/All that I need (general)	11	3	29
	(46)	(32)	(14)*

* Caution Low Base

Table 7.7 Familiarity with Brands. Reprinted with permission from Samsung

	Samsung		Philips		Nokia	
	Exposed	Not Exposed	Exposed	Not Exposed	Exposed	Not Exposed
Extremely familiar	12	12	11	13	20	12
Very familiar	23	17	22	17	31	33
Familiar	43	44	35	34	29	37
Slightly familiar	11	13	15	21	12	11
Know only by name	11	13	17	14	8	6
Don't Know	0	1	1	1	1	1

Base: Total sample

Table 7.8 Consideration Scale. Reprinted with permission from Samsung

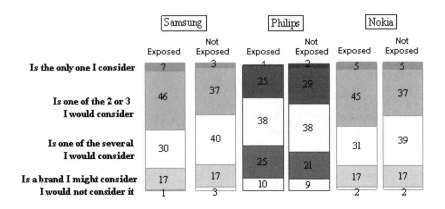

Base Total

Table 7.9 Key Measures for Samsung – Monitors. Reprinted with permission from Samsung

	Exposed %	Not Exposed %	Sponsorship Contribution
Spontaneous Brand Awareness Top of Mind	33	23	+10
Spontaneous Brand Awareness Total Mentions	52	41	+11
Would Consider on Next Purchase	63	32	+31
Brand Favourability	33	17	+16
Familiarity	35	29	+6
Publicity Awareness	89	63	+26

Brand Image

Table 7.10 Brand Image Profile. Reprinted with permission from Samsung

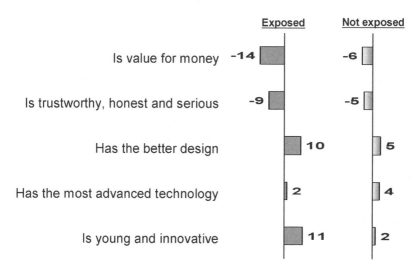

Table 7.11 Advertising Awareness and Media Recall. Reprinted with permission from Samsung

Saw Advertising %		TV %	Radio %	Newspaper %	Sponsorship / Events %	Internet %	Outdoor Media * %	Mailing %	Magazines %	Word of Mouth %
50	LG	60	8	38	21	38	32	5	63	33
53	Motorola	63	11	38	26	23	42	5	61	32
67	Nokia	80	17	47	25	32	40	7	68	35
41	Philips	81	20	39	27	25	36	4	65	25
76	Samsung	71	15	35	68	29	39	10	65	35
4	TCE *	31	23	31	8	8	8	8	54	23

Base: Total Sample (300)
* Caution: Low Base

Overall rating of the event

- 'I thought it was great; it gave [me] the opportunity to meet new people, to learn about the Samsung devices. I saw athletes.'
- 'I think it had a good structure. It valorized the Samsung brand. The presentation of the products was very creative and the event made the beach cheerful.'
- 'I thought it was great. It was free and open to the public. The people got in touch with the players. It was well organized. It had information about the games. The people who worked at the event were well instructed [about it] and provided a lot of information about the games and it had a lot of security.'
- 'I expected it would have more volleyball players and I expected it would have soccer on the sand, but it didn't. I didn't like the bands.'
- 'I thought the event was very interesting because it was a sports event, but the event was too élite-oriented. The [general public] had no access to the event because the tickets were too expensive.'

Summary of Results

The above graphs and tables provided Samsung with valuable indicators regarding the success of their sponsorship in terms of the consumers' enjoyment of the event and the effect that it had on their awareness and perception of the Samsung brand.

By splitting the sample into those 'exposed' vs. those 'not exposed' one is able to isolate what the sponsorship contributed towards the brand in terms of awareness, consideration, favourability and familiarity. Some of the most positive results are as follows:

- In terms of generating awareness, the sponsorship is more effective for Samsung mobile phones than for Samsung monitors. For mobile phones, the contribution of sponsorship was +15 per cent for top of mind awareness and +32 per cent for total brand awareness whereas for monitors it was +10 per cent and +11 per cent respectively.

- As a brand for monitors, where Samsung already enjoys a leadership position, consideration for next purchase and favourability ratings grew by almost 100 per cent amongst the exposed respondents.

- As a mobile phone brand, the sponsorship had a considerable impact on consideration to purchase with a +29 per cent difference amongst those exposed vs. those not exposed.

- The biggest contribution of the sponsorship on image of the brand Samsung was bringing youthfulness and innovation. Design is also a standout among the exposed.

- The event itself was very well evaluated with 70 per cent of respondents classifying it as very good and saying that it was well organized, great, had lots of leisure options and good access to the internet.

- 17 per cent of people mentioned the product stands (with products being shown and demonstrated) as a positive aspect of the event.

- The attendees were in line with the Samsung target – i.e. men and women, the majority between the ages of 16–30 years.

KEY INSIGHT

By establishing specific objectives upfront and using sponsorship evaluation tools that isolated the effect of the sponsorship on brand awareness, image, consideration and favourability, Samsung could truly measure the impact of the sponsorship. Furthermore, Samsung had actionable data around which it could formulate tactical and strategic planning for the next sponsorship cycle.

Measurement guidelines

There are some basic guidelines that should be followed when developing a passion branding measurement methodology and then evaluating it.

First and foremost, measurement should be integrated into the overall management of the passion branding campaign as was highlighted in Chapter 6 and most importantly budgeted for up front. A 2002 IEG study conducted by Performance Research amongst 200 top decision-makers highlighted that 78 per cent of respondents do not have an ongoing budget dedicated to sponsorship research. 72 per cent reported that that they allocate either nothing or no more than 1 per cent of their sponsorship budgets to concurrent or post-event research.

Secondly, measure against a benchmark established at the commencement of the campaign. There is no point in getting to the end of the campaign before trying to establish measurement objectives. Added to this is the need to establish the measurement criteria up front so that there is no ambiguity or conflict created around the basis upon which the campaign will be measured.

Thirdly, the objectives that you set up front should be detailed and specific as well as being measurable, e.g.: 'our key objective is to increase purchase consideration of our brand amongst black males 18–24 years in the Northeast from 12 per cent to 25 per cent'. The more tightly the objective is defined the easier it will be to measure against it.

Fourthly, where appropriate, borrow proven measurement tools and techniques from other areas of the marketing and communication industry such as media measurement for broadcast sponsorships. Do not however be sucked into trying to use measures that really do not have any relevance simply because, for example, you want to try and compare passion branding to traditional above-the-line advertising.

Fifthly, if at all possible, try and curtail other promotional activity during the period in which your passion branding campaign is up and running. Back yourself and passion branding and in the process you will be able to more clearly define the effect of your passion branding campaign. If you find this impossible to do, then in your research look at trying to separate the responses of consumers exposed to your passion branding campaign from those not exposed. In the process, you should be able to get a pretty good read as to how effective your passion branding campaign has been.

Finally, try to talk to as many people as possible about the passion branding campaign. The greatest insight often comes from simply speaking to the people that you interact with on a daily basis. Take this one step further by insisting that you and your team spend time talking to your consumers in the places where they consume either your brand or the passion that you've adopted to market off. I understand that Unilever now requires this of all their marketing people and are most encouraged by the greater insight that their teams now have into their consumers and the things that are important to them.

As I said at the beginning of this chapter, passion branding measurement will never be a science so do not try to turn it into one. This is particularly the case when it comes to the evaluation of the results thrown up by your measurement. Take the quantitative and qualitative results and blend them together with a good dose of common sense to give you an overall sense as to the direction you are heading and to highlight the areas of the campaign that you need to concentrate on going forward.

Leading Thought
Sean O'Neill, *Brand and Market Communication Director, Diageo*

I believe that measurement and evaluation is the single most important challenge facing the sponsorship industry. I also believe that it's the biggest opportunity.

Delivery of A&P (advertising and promotions) effectiveness is a critical driver of brand growth and brand profitability, so step one in the measurement and evaluation process is to ensure that there is a culture within your organization which accepts the need for measurement and values the information (both positive and negative) which it will deliver.

Step two is to set very clear, measurable and attainable objectives. Sponsorship can't do everything, so make sure you understand sponsorship well enough and the entity you're sponsoring well enough to be able to know that it can deliver against your expectations.

Once you've established that, measurement becomes simple because you know precisely what you're measuring whether it's new recruits, awareness, incremental volume, perception shifts – no matter what.

Within Diageo, we have some very sophisticated measurement models for all the elements associated with brand health and equity such as image dimensions, relevance or consumer attitudes. We also have great models for measuring the success of our promotions, advertising and PR. All of these models can be adapted for use against sponsorship when we set objectives in these areas.

For example, one of the goals you might set a sponsorship is the task of increasing the consumer scores against the statement 'this brand is a brand for people like me'. If that's the case, it's that objective that will help shape the type of exploitation play that you run and that's what you measure.

When you look at the research that is done either by event owners or sponsorship companies it will tell you that when you ask consumers 'are you more likely to purchase one of this company's products because they sponsor this team or event?' the answer is always yes. Now to me that is almost meaningless because consumers feel that they should say yes to the question. I genuinely don't see too much value in asking that question, and even less in using it as a reason for rights owners and agencies to help sell sponsorship.

I think the only true way of evaluating a response to that question is by looking at the consumer that you want to engage through your sponsorship. Then, track them through the sponsorship and beyond (particularly if it's a sponsorship over time) and see how their relationship with the brand has changed.

In Rugby World Cup we were able to do that in Britain and Ireland and Australia by looking at the promotions we'd done around rugby, both in bars and the off-trade, and doing selected sample follow-ups over time to confirm the impact that event had had on them.

So I don't think it's because you sponsor that consumers will indicate a greater propensity to buy or consume your product. I think it's the way in which you explore the association and how you make it relevant to consumers that will determine whether they do indeed buy and consume your brands.

Measurement Tools

There are any number of these tools, and a growing number at that.

In response to the growing need for reliable measurement tools, Octagon in South Africa, with the help of the country's leading media agency Nota Bene, have developed a passion branding evaluation tool, which we've called *evalu8*. The model uses input from recognized local measurement agencies including Sponsor Statistik and Median.

Evalu8 can be used for both pre- and post-analysis, to help in the selection of suitable passion branding platforms, to value a passion branding campaign's return on investment or evaluate if a campaign has been effectively leveraged or not and the desired effect achieved. *Evalu8* can be used to evaluate broadcast and programme sponsorships (television and radio), event sponsorships, sponsorships of teams and individuals, causes and other passion platforms.

Evalu8 considers passion branding as a process and evaluates it through an analysis of strategic fit, media exposure (which includes broadcast sponsorship, 'free' media PR and incidental logo coverage), the effect of the sponsorship on the sponsoring brand (brand linkage, attribute transfer, propensity to purchase), the business effect and finally use of the platform and the rights package made available by the passion platform.

Evalu8 is not intended as a 'fix-all' tool but rather as something that will assist passion branders in assessing what is important and then assigning some element of measurement to those areas.

Evalu8 – a sponsorship evaluation tool[1]

1. Strategic fit assessment

The starting point should always be to assess the strategic fit of the passion branding platform and the sponsoring brand because if the fit and alignment are not right then the sponsorship is not worth doing in the first place.

One needs to ask, is the sponsorship aligned in terms of Figure 7.1:

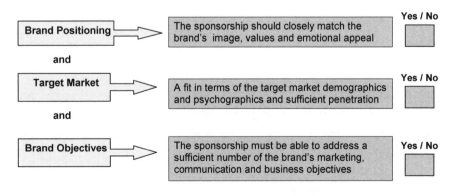

---

[1]   These extracts from *evalu8* have been reproduced here with permission of Nota Bene, Jim Taylor and Erica Dreijer in particular and Octagon South Africa.

2. Media exposure

Media exposure is a good indication of a sponsorship's visibility and is an effective medium through which to communicate the basic sponsorship proposition or message thereby generating awareness. It is therefore an important first step if the rest of the sponsoring brand's objectives are to be met.

2.1. Broadcast Sponsorship

Broadcast sponsorships typically provide the greatest measurable return for a sponsor. In order to accurately determine the value one should consider both the cost-efficiency of the inventory received as part of the package (e.g. billboards, stings, on-screen logo, etc.) as well as the creative execution as this can have a material impact on the consumer's awareness of the association in terms of communicating the appropriateness of the sponsorship in the consumer's mind.

The value of the sponsorship inventory should at the very least equal the broadcast sponsorship cost. If it does not then either the sponsorship cost, or the amount of inventory received, must be re-negotiated. The creative execution of the broadcast elements should increase the value to anything from 1.2 to 1.5 times the cost of the sponsorship.

2.2. Branding exposure

This measures the incidental brand logotype exposure received on television whether it be during live broadcasts or exposure via news bulletins or other inserts. This is done using a calculation that takes into account four factors relating to the broadcast.

- Total brand exposure time.
- Total broadcast time.
- Frequency (number of times the brand/logo came into view).
- Viewership.

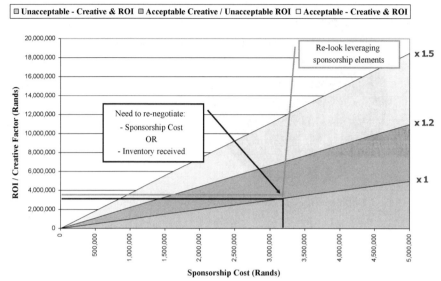

Figure 7.2 *Evalu8* Broadcast Sponsorship analysis. Reprinted with permission from NotaBene

The most widely recognized tool to measure this exposure is the **Spindex**® monitoring tool, developed by S-Comm, a network of independently owned and managed companies in 10 countries around the world. **Spindex**® arrives at a value for the exposure through its Spindex point which is a combination of the above four factors as well as research which looks at the recall factor of various branded elements relative to the recall of perimeter boards. Refer to Figures 7.3 and 7.4.

This measure allows one to compare the exposure across different sponsored properties and platforms as well as across the different branded items e.g. billboards vs. clothing etc.

2.3. Media PR analysis

Evalu8 measures the volume of media exposure and ascribes an equivalent advertising rate card value to it. *Evalu8* then aims to extract the wastage to value only that exposure which reached the desired target audience. In addition, *Evalu8* can analyse exposure at any number of levels, from

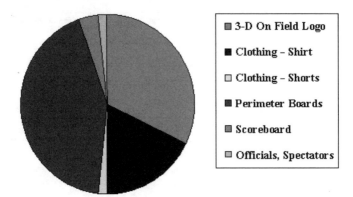

Figure 7.3 Spindex® comparison by branded item

Figure 7.4 Spindex® comparison by sponsored platform

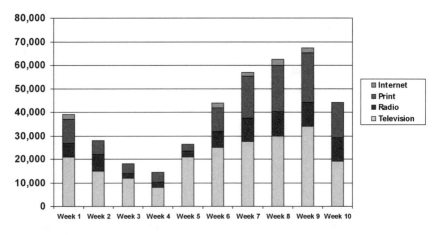

Figure 7.5 Weekly spread of media coverage per medium

exposure by week, by region, by journalist, by publication/radio station/ television programme, by tonality etc. all of which can identify specific insights that are actionable rather than serve merely as a reference for the sponsoring brand. More importantly, *evalu8*'s analysis looks at the extent to which the sponsor's desired messaging came through in the media exposure. Refer to Figures 7.5 and 7.6.

3. Brand effect

Media based evaluations only report that the sponsor's message has been sent out and how many times it has been sent out but do not indicate whether or not the brand message has been received and what action, if any, has been taken by the target market as a result of that message. This requires further analysis, usually in the form of both qualitative and quantitative consumer analysis which can establish:

- The consumer's awareness of the link between the sponsored property and the brand.
- The consumer's response to the sponsorship in terms of what it conveys to them about the brand – image attribute transfer.
- The impact of the sponsorship on the consumer's relationship with the brand in terms of brand perceptions, brand loyalty and propensity to purchase.

The most accurate way of gauging the true impact of the sponsorship as opposed to other communication channels, is to isolate the responses of those consumers who were exposed to the sponsorship against those consumers who were not exposed to the sponsorship and to note the differential.

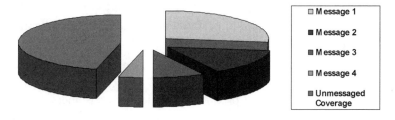

Figure 7.6 Sponsor messaging exposure

This research must be tailored to the specific brand attributes and objectives of the sponsor and can determine which sponsorship elements had the greatest effect on consumer attitudes and which were least effective.

3.1. Brand health – image attribute transfer
See Figure 7.7.

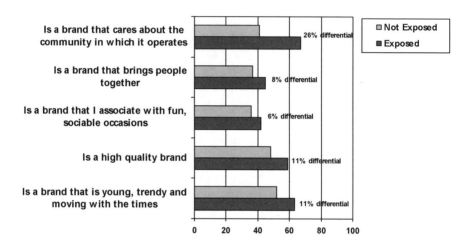

Figure 7.7 Brand image attributes

3.2. Propensity to purchase
To what extent, if any, does the sponsorship increase one's propensity to purchase the sponsoring brand rather than a competitor's product? Refer to Figure 7.8.

4. Business effect

The ability of a sponsorship to directly impact on the bottom line is becoming an increasingly important deliverable and must be built into the evaluation process where relevant.

Business related objectives can include the sponsorship's ability to:

- increased sales or use of a product or service by consumers.
- drive sales to business customers (business to business relationships).
- increase the number of distribution outlets.

- increase the sponsor's client portfolio.
- generate more product display space at point-of-sale.
- identify specific targeted qualified new leads.

The tracking mechanism used will depend on the type of business related objective that is desired by the sponsor. The tracking should aim to isolate the effect of the sponsorship on the sales increase.

5. Sponsorship Property Evaluation

The greater the extent to which the consumers' passions are leveraged through the sponsorship platform, the more effective the sponsorship's contribution can be towards building the brand and driving sales.

Evalu8 assesses various elements that relate to the sponsored property and the extent to which they were maximized by the sponsor.

5.1. Rights inventory

A rights inventory gives an assessment of the rights package acquired by the sponsor in terms of their relevance to the sponsor's objectives and the extent to which the sponsor utilized them effectively.

5.2. Quality of the opportunity

This is an assessment of the sponsored property in terms of the credibility of the rights owner, sponsor clutter, prestige of the association and rights owner initiated marketing campaigns.

Table 7.8 Evalu8 purchase measurement

Statement	Exposed	Not Exposed	% Differential
It will contribute significantly	64%	21%	43%
It will contribute somewhat	24%	17%	7%
It will not influence my purchase behaviour	12%	62%	−50%

Note: Information provided is fictitious and for sample purposes only

Table 7.9 Evalu8 sales measurement

	Target	Actual
Overall Sales during sponsorship period	$1 000 000	$1 100 000
Uptake of sponsorship themed promotion	+5%	+6%

Note: Information provided is fictitious and for sample purposes only

5.3. Execution/event analysis

This analysis gives an assessment of particular attributes of the event and the consumer's overall attitude towards, and enjoyment of, their experience at the sponsored event. Evaluation is tailored to address the specific activation tactics which were used in the execution of the sponsorship. It is also worth evaluating what consumers considered the tactics demonstrated about the sponsoring brand (Note that this is closely linked to the brand effect evaluation discussed in Section 3).

This section in particular can provide worthwhile insights that can be applied to improve the sponsorship in the next cycle and it therefore makes sense to use open-ended questions that will elicit richer responses.

Some possible questions that could be asked:

- What did you like about this event?
- What didn't you like about this event?
- What differentiates this event from other [name of sport] events?
- What aspects of the marketing/leveraging of this event had the greatest impact on you?

Applying the Evalu8 Formula

Evalu8 is equipped to arrive at a value for the overall sponsorship by adopting a widely accepted valuation model used to value companies, namely the price/earnings ratio model in which the sustainable earnings of a business is multiplied by a multiple determined by taking into account the earnings growth potential of the company relative to the market, i.e. Value = PE multiple × sustainable earnings. The PE multiple is determined by taking an industry or category average and adjusting this based on various subjective factors in the eyes of the buyer.

If this is applied in the context of sponsorship, the sustainable earnings refer to the measurable benefits of a sponsorship (i.e. those to which a monetary value can be directly ascribed), and the PE multiple refers to 'non measurable benefits' (i.e. those elements to which it is difficult to ascribe a straight financial value). The PE multiple is referred to as the *Evalu8* Factor.

Identifying problem areas that require interaction

Apart from its value in assessing the suitability of a potential passion platform or the effectiveness of a campaign post-campaign, measurement can play a very meaningful role in the ongoing management of a passion branding campaign.

The trick is to set up the measurement of key performance areas in such a way that the results can be timeously assessed as required during the campaign as opposed to three months after the campaign when it's too late to do anything about any problems identified until the next cycle of the sponsorship. This requires almost daily monitoring but the investment can be well worth the effort. There may however be certain measurement methodologies, which do not provide the necessary flexibility.

The first example of this relates to media monitoring. By having the media monitored on an ongoing basis, it will be possible to identify journalists or media owners for example that seem to be reporting negatively towards a passion branding campaign or some element of it. By being made aware of this fact as it starts to become evident an effort can be made to address the problem and improve the relationship between the sponsoring brand and the journalist or media owner concerned before it is too late and more damage is done.

Similarly, where a certain publication or station appears not to be covering the event or sponsored activity, then an extra focus can be placed on this publication to try and rectify the situation. This all happens while the project is 'live' as opposed to only finding out about the problem when it is all over.

A second example relates to the leverage communication that is put in place around a passion platform. By testing the efficacy or liking of the communication both in advance of, and during, the campaign any problems can be identified as early on as possible and an effort made to correct the problem before the show is over.

8

A changing landscape –
some challenges to manage

The evolution of delivery platforms

As marketers and techno-buffs start to work closer together to deliver new technology that focuses not just on technological development but rather on customer needs and wants, the number of delivery platforms that exist will start to increase exponentially.

With the emergence of satellite television, we have all witnessed firsthand the explosion in the number of television channels available to viewers who, as a result, have more choice and are therefore more difficult for marketers to track down.

We have not heard the last of the role of the internet in all of this. The convergence of television and the internet will, when it sorts itself out technologically, on the one hand become the greatest audience splitter ever seen whilst on the other the most efficient mechanism yet seen for those wanting to reach a niche market. I am not saying *when* this is all going to happen but you can be sure it going to.

And then there's TIVO, the personal video recorder or PVT, which allows users to pause live TV, fast forward through ads, record their favourite shows (two at the same time off different channels) and the like – basically, take full control of what they see and when they see it.

Although still in its infancy, when mature, TIVO technology will have such a significant impact on the way that people consume television that it will force a change in the way in which marketers use television to reach certain audiences. In a world where consumers are becoming 'turned off' to interruption-marketing like traditional advertising, TIVO must surely have the potential to become a mass-market phenomenon.

So what does all this mean for the passion brander? Well, it is actually good news because programme content will become more important than ever. Passion branding's strength as a permission marketing tool and its ability to place a sponsoring brand alongside or as part of that content in an open and transparent way will become more valuable then ever. Viewers will not want to, or be able to for that matter, 'Tivo' your brand and/or messages from what they watch because you will have become part of the content that they consume, part of their passion.

Leading Thought
Harlan Stone, *Velocity Sports & Entertainment*

Sponsorships will clearly be affected by the overall changing of the advertising model – as the 30 and 60 second commercial become less and less valuable *and* as media fragmentation continues, advertising-driven sponsorships will come under more and more scrutiny and more grass roots 'unzappable' sponsorship efforts will be important.

From an overall standpoint I think we are witnessing the disappearance of 'tweeners' – i.e. either a sponsorship will be very big/global or at least national in scope and include big time 'event' television (where consumers tend not to zap the commercials) or we will find that sponsorships of smaller 'niche' events, that don't rely on any television but instead have a direct-to-consumer grass roots reach, will become more prevalent. Events in the middle i.e. non-significant tennis, golf, rugby, cricket etc. will tend to have a much harder time attracting sponsorship but the championships – Wimbledon, World Cup, etc. – will continue to thrive.

Traditional sports business models under threat

The heady days of the 1990s in the sports industry are but a memory – well, that is what I believe at any rate.

The last decade of the 20th century saw an all out battle between media owners wanting to use sport as a platform off which to launch their offering to a sports crazy public. This had the effect of driving up television rights fees to unbelievable levels and more distressingly created some very bloated sports federations and sports property owners who now pay their athletes too much money.

There is however currently a correction in play that is going to dramatically change the business model in the world of professional sport with some significant fallout as a result.

Firstly, the competition between broadcasters for television rights is no longer going to be as intense as it has been. As a result, this market is going to be more of a buyer's market than a seller's market and 'marginal' rights are going to have to settle for much less money than they have become used to. Despite this, demand for top quality rights will remain strong so we can expect to see the television rights market mirroring the situation that we have in the world economy where the differential between the 'haves and the have nots' will continue to grow.

Secondly, the mix of funding enjoyed by sports federations and sports property owners is going to change. As television rights revenues start to fall so they will have to start to look in other areas for replacement funding. Sponsorship will be one of the first areas that they'll turn to. The problem here is that existing sponsors won't be interested in increasing their sponsorships unless the owners can demonstrate an increased value return which is not always going to be possible. The owners will therefore be tempted to try and increase the number of sponsors that they take on board which will have the effect of potentially diluting the value enjoyed by existing sponsors.

Another area in which new revenue will be sought will include ticketing which will require that the owners find ways of attracting the spectators back to their events which is going to be easier said than done and will require that most of them take their game to a higher level.

All new avenues will need to be pursued from strategic partnerships with suppliers, e.g., sharing call line revenue on information and competition lines with cellular network providers, travel agencies offering travel packages to sporting events, financial service providers offering life insurance policies to fans, etc. All in all, more clutter!

It is not all bad news for sponsors however, particularly those that are prepared to stand up to the plate and make a bigger investment in their sponsorship. Just as the large rights fee-paying broadcasters have come to have a fair amount of influence over the sports federations and properties that they support so too will the opportunity exist for the savvy sponsor to do the same.

Thirdly, the cost structures of the sports federations and sports properties most affected will need to change with player costs likely to be the first port of call. As a result, the huge player packages that have become common place in most professional sport will rather become the exception than the rule.

Leading Thought
Karl Bistany, *Managing Director for Europe, Africa and Australasia and President of Television for Octagon Worldwide*

The model is definitely going to change as the high revenues from television of the past start to dry up.

So, if for the sake of argument, the ratio of revenues were, 50 per cent television, 25 per cent tickets, 25 per cent sponsorship, then I think that ratio will end up within 12 months, where television will drop down to, for the sake of argument, 30 per cent, corporate sponsorship will go up to 30–40 per cent and the balance will be ticket sales. This of course will not apply to premium properties such as the Olympics, international football (World Cup and European Championships) and their equivalents in other sports.

In this new environment, the role of the corporate provider, the corporate sponsorship provider, is going to increase in importance. If the sports bodies are intelligent they will say 'okay we understand that the world's changed, it's moved on, we need more money generally, we can't increase the television money because that was at the height of the market – what we can do, is demand more of the sponsors but only if we give them more by way of integrated marketing programmes, through local, regional and, where appropriate, global leveraging and by addressing a client's particular needs'. Most sports bodies however don't understand that, let alone have the expertise to deliver it.

As the revenues from television start to dry up so too will the new/ renewed player contracts as has been the case in Europe with the football market which is a good example of how it went through the roof. The number of transfers have dropped by 20–30 per cent in terms of volume but also there have been few high value transfers and by that I mean transfers north of US$20 million, we've only seen two or three to be honest.

So to summarize the business model is going forward. As they pay less for rights, broadcasters are going to have less influence than they have had up until now (relatively speaking); corporates meanwhile will start to have a greater influence but will expect more in return, and players will probably have to accept on average that they're going to earn less than they have over the last 10 years but none-the-less still live like kings.

Leading Thought
Chuck Fruit, *Senior Vice President, The Coca-Cola Company*

I started in sports marketing about 25 years ago. At that point in time, the headlines were that the sports business model is broken, that TV rights fees cannot continue to escalate at this rate, and that a totally new model is required. Well, guess what? Twenty-five years later the headlines continue to predict gloom and doom for the sports and sponsorship business. And yet we haven't even reached the point yet where consumer subscription TV and pay-per-view revenues represent significant income for teams and leagues. I believe new technologies will continue to open up new revenue streams for the sports business via pay-per-view, TV season tickets, etc.

Ultimately the consumers pay for everything. So the question would seem to be, 'have we saturated consumer desire for access and interaction with their favourite sports?' My guess is the answer is 'no', and as long as we haven't saturated that demand, and they're willing to pay for that access and interaction, there's lots of opportunities to grow sports revenues.

Leading Thought
Iain Banner, *Chief Executive, Laureus World Sports Awards*

We've already seen the substantial change in the television rights market. This is going to dramatically change the revenue model for many sports property owners. Commercial rights will become even more important, with television becoming the platform that gives rights value rather than direct income. The most important thing will be understanding the product and the needs and potential of that product. On the activation side, for many brands, less exposure but more loyalty evolution will be a target.

Increased television revenues have resulted in the player being overpaid. There's been a direct correlation between rights fees and what people get paid and that's going to have to adjust. It needs real adjusting. It's very simple – there's been an overstatement of income and an overstatement of expenditure so the expenditure is going to have to be cut. Significantly, cuts will have to come from what are turning out to be outrageous player fees. Television will no longer necessarily buy rights but rather make air time available to rights holders who will package product up to take advantage of that air time, for the benefit of advertisers and sponsors. This should be good for sponsors.

With respect to attendances, the on field packaging will have to be evaluated. If promoters communicate relevantly with their audience and on field performance is enhanced through individual flair and team performance, then they're going to start getting people to watch again.

It's a natural cycle. I see things changing but I think it's a natural cycle and in a sense, the flow of funds has corrupted sport a lot. I think the sponsor will be there as one moves forward and in fact the sponsor will probably become more and more important in the future.

Increasing sponsorship clutter

As with all good things in life, when discovered by the masses they tend to lose some of their shine. In passion branding's case, the discovery of the power of this marketing medium will give rise over time to increasing clutter – more and more brands trying to get in on the act. Sponsorship currently comprises on average between 10 per cent and 12 per cent of marketing budgets but as smart marketers start to see the value in sponsorship this figure can be expected to double and then double again over the next ten to fifteen years.

This increasing clutter will force up the cost of associating with premium properties and send passion branders in search of new platforms which are, as yet, unexposed or unexploited. Subsequently the passion brander will be able to own a premium space but this will require that they become more creative with their ideas both in terms of what they sponsor and more importantly how they leverage their association.

Leading Thought
David Butler, *Head of Laureus Sport For Good Foundation and Manager of Laureus World Sports Academy*

There will continue to be the broadening gulf between 'have' and 'have not' sports which will continue to create a handful of highly successful sporting platforms tied to television. Within those platforms there will be a continuing gap between those who are at the top and those who struggle in terms of performance and commercial value. Unsuccessful teams will continue to fall away and this in turn will have an adverse effect on sporting codes as a whole which will lead to a pressure to match performance and commercial needs.

Essentially, it's more of the same though the wheel will eventually turn. New generation sports such as extreme and boarding will continue to emerge to change the sporting landscape. Big sports will price themselves out of the market and find themselves losing consumer interest if they are not able to deliver the basic product: competitive and exciting sporting endeavour.

As sports become expensive global platforms, they will only really be of value to big global brands looking to make big global positioning statements. Macro sponsorships will therefore need to provide real entrées and real points of difference in order to be commercially viable and give effective returns.

As the big fish grow bigger, more and more sponsors will seek opportunities amongst the little fish, creating unique points of difference by adopting and integrating platforms into their brands through innovation and touching niche communities relevant to product.

Big fish: big spend, little fish: big IDEAS.

Generation Y

Generation Y is the largest generation to make its presence felt since the baby boomers and they are more different than any other generation before them.

In the United States, Generation Y is already 60 million strong and more than three times the size of Generation X. In South Africa, by way of example, Generation Y accounts for almost a quarter of the population and when fully developed will account for 35 per cent of the population, double the size of the local boomer generation.

Not only is this market important for what it will become in time but it is equally important for what it is right now, a market that has great influence over family spending patterns as well as their own discretionary spending. For example, America's YTV *Tween Report* showed that 9–14 year olds influence their parent's choice of just about everything including cars and computers.

Generation Y therefore provides probably the most exciting marketing opportunity yet seen for the passion brander that is able to read this generation's passions right and understand them best.

In fact, I would go as far as to say that any passion brander that does not make it their business to get to know this market extremely well will be missing out on a huge immediate opportunity. Their interests and passions are different to the mainstream passions and interests that we adults feel comfortable with. Despite this, the rules of engagement are the same as those outlined in this book – it is just the passion platforms that you use may be different.

More importantly however, today's 'tweeners' will become tomorrow's adults and are expected to potentially change the broader dynamics of society over the next ten to twenty years. If you don't get to know them now, you may well never!

Ambush marketing

Long the pariah of the sponsorship industry, ambush marketing[1] is at last starting to be taken seriously by governments around the world who are

---

[1] The attempt by a non-sponsor to capitalize on the popularity or prestige of an event or property by giving the false impression that it is a sponsor. This kind of activity is often employed by the competitors of a property's official sponsor.

now increasingly starting to introduce legislation to protect against it and apply stringent penalties against those responsible for this unethical approach to marketing.

The International Olympic Committee must take a lot of credit for having led the charge in this fight as is evident from the onerous, yet vital, anti-ambush marketing obligations that it places on cities hosting its Summer and Winter Games. Having been exposed in Atlanta in 1996, the IOC quickly moved to restore the confidence of its commercial partners in Nagano, Sydney and Salt Lake City and in the process add further value to its offering.

Other world sports bodies have followed the IOC's lead and there appears generally to be a move towards embracing the principles established by the IOC which is good news for the sponsorship industry in general and should give sponsors additional comfort that ambush marketing is something which their partners have recognized and are keen to see limited if not eradicated all together.

What is also encouraging is that a number of brands that previously utilized ambush marketing as part and parcel of their marketing and communication strategies, like Nike for example, seem to have recognized the error in their ways and a degree of self regulation amongst the leading brands is starting to become evident with the guiding principle being one of do unto others as you would have done unto yourself.

A few words of warning though. Care should be taken by these bodies not to alienate their fans in the process of implementing and policing ambush marketing. A case in point was the 2003 ICC Cricket World Cup in South Africa which I believe took the issue too far. The organizing committee took the position ahead of the event that fans would not be permitted to bring competitor products, or wear clothing advertising the official sponsor's rivals, into the stadia.

Anti-ambush marketing activities need to be handled with sensitivity where the fans' experience at the event is concerned and will be of little value to passion branders if the activities end up alienating the very people that they are trying to connect with. I experienced the negative impact of Cricket World Cup's policy first hand when a fan in front of me at the security checkpoint at the final of the event had the label of her bottle of

Valpre water removed by the security guard, much to her annoyance and disbelief, simply because it was produced by a competitor of Pepsi's. I wonder what she thinks of Pepsi now?

Leading Thought
Lawrence Flanagan, *Executive Vice President and Chief Marketing Officer for Global Marketing, MasterCard International*

Probably the biggest danger, I would say, dealing with any of the major sports leagues, is their ability to protect their sponsor's rights. The ambush potential of the individual teams breaking off, defying the league rules and doing their own local sponsorships is a real concern. This kind of behaviour would be very damaging as it would really blow the integrity of the whole sponsorship model, as we know it, apart.

As a matter of policy we don't do any ambush marketing but rather take the high road in all our sponsorship activities.

Appendix

Thought leaders' pen pictures

The following Thought Leaders have contributed either directly or indirectly to some of the thinking behind *Passion Branding*. Together, they represent a huge reservoir of knowledge on the subject of passion branding and I am greatly indebted to them for having taken the time to share their thoughts with me.

Iain Banner

Iain is CEO and co-founder of Laureus World Sports Awards Limited and Director of Sponsorship for the Richemont Group. Based on the vision of founder Johann Rupert, Iain developed the concept and business plan for the Laureus World Sports Awards and initiated the joint venture between founding patrons Richemont and DaimlerChrysler to fund and support the concept. Iain is now responsible for implementing Rupert's vision. Prior to joining Richemont in 1994, Iain was a Director and Partner of the Gary Player Group.

Karl Bistany

Karl joined CSI over 10 years ago as a Manager in Technical Services. Previously Karl had been learning the sports rights trade at the Middle Eastern agency, Trans World Television (TWT). Since that time Karl's role within the organization has continued to grow, becoming Sales Manager, General Manager and then Chief Executive of the organization.

Since CSI became part of the Octagon Group in February 1998, Karl has been working very closely with the parent company to develop new business for Octagon CSI and the rest of the Group, as well as being ultimately responsible for overseeing all television interests worldwide. In February 2002 Karl was appointed Managing Director for Europe, Africa and Australasia and President of Television for Octagon Worldwide.

Michael Brockbank

Michael Brockbank joined Unilever in October 1989. Following a number of assignments as advertising specialist on specific Unilever food brands, he is now Vice President Brand Communication, with the mission to improve the return on the investment made by Unilever in the communication of all leading brands.

Previously he had spent 20 years with J. Walter Thompson, half in the UK, half in the Netherlands. He was Vice President of JWT and Client Service Director of their Dutch office.

Michael's agency career included both account management and advertising planning functions worldwide, as well as local responsibilities. He handled Unilever accounts both in the UK and in Holland, working with detergents and personal products companies. Besides Unilever, his list of international food and drink clients included Nestlé, Kellogg's, Sara Lee, RHM, Beechams and Hero.

David Butler

Since graduating from Oxford where he sports-edited the prestigious *Cherwell* and read an honours degree in history, David Butler has travelled the world of sport and sports marketing living in Sydney, Cape Town and London.

Communications Manager for Cape Town's 2004 Olympic bid at the age of 26, David returned to South Africa having managed British Athletics' sponsor communications for three years as Media Director of the highly successful 1997 Lions Tour.

He subsequently headed media for Octagon in South Africa working extensively with a number of leading blue chip clients before setting up Etv national sports news as Director of Octagon television and editorially creating and producing several shows for the SABC and Etv.

He started Octagon's first interactive division in 2000.

Returning to London, David now travels the world as Head of the Laureus Sport for Good Foundation and Manager of the Laureus World Sports Academy.

He is a contributing editor for *GQ* magazine, is publishing his first children's novel in 2003 and is an avid boxer.

Lawrence Flanagan

Lawrence Flanagan is Executive Vice President and Chief Marketing Officer, Global Marketing, for MasterCard International where he has primary responsibility for the strategic, consumer-focused evolution and management of the MasterCard® brand and the company's various consumer-branded payment solutions.

To accomplish his objectives, Larry utilizes advertising development, internet marketing, sponsorships, promotional programmes, integrated marketing communications, global research and statistics, and other initiatives.

Using an integrated marketing approach, MasterCard successfully leverages its advertising, sponsorships, and promotional programmes across its major global markets. The company's highly acclaimed Priceless® advertising campaign is currently airing in more than 80 countries worldwide and has earned numerous awards and honours, including a Gold Effie, an Addy Award, and The Cresta. MasterCard is proud sponsor of the world's leading sports events and organizations, including World Cup soccer, Major League Baseball®, the PGA Tour®, PGA of America®, National Hockey League®, and Jordan Grand Prix Formula One team.

Larry previously held the titles of Senior Vice President, North America Marketing, and Vice President, US Advertising. Larry joined MasterCard in October 1996 from L'Oreal, where he was Assistant Vice President, Marketing, for the company's U.S. Cosmetic and Fragrance Division. In this capacity, Larry led the repositioning of the Plenitude Skin Care line of products; he also played a key role in the purchase and re-organization of the well-known Maybelline brand by L'Oreal in 1996.

From 1986 through 1994, Larry held various marketing positions for Procter & Gamble's Beauty Care Division, where he was ultimately responsible for all marketing initiatives in support of the Cover Girl Cosmetics brand, as Marketing Director. Larry also played a key role in the acquisition of the Shulton and Max Factor brands.

Larry holds a Bachelor of Science degree from the University of New Haven.

Charles B. Fruit

Chuck Fruit is Senior Vice President, Worldwide Media and Alliances for the Coca-Cola Company where he is responsible for the development of worldwide media strategies and the Company's investments in all forms of traditional and emerging media platforms. Included in these responsibilities is the direction of Coca-Cola business relationships with the major media, entertainment, and sports organizations around the world. Also under his direction are the US media planning and buying functions for all of the company's operating units and its brand-building programmes with leading entertainment and sports properties.

Chuck began his career with the company in June 1991 as Director of Global Media Services and was elected Vice President in July 1991. He was given expanded responsibilities and named Vice President, Media & Marketing Assets in August 1993. He served as Marketing Chief of Staff beginning in November 2000 and named to his current position in October 2001.

Prior to joining The Coca-Cola Company, Chuck spent 15 years at Anheuser-Busch, Inc., where he held a variety of positions including Vice President of Corporate Media and Sports Marketing, as well as President of Busch Media Group, Inc., the company's in-house media planning and buying subsidiary. Previously, he was with Gardner Advertising Company in St. Louis where he was Vice President of the agency's media/planning subsidiary.

Chuck received a bachelor's degree from Williams College in Williamstown, Massachusetts and has been an active participant in advertising industry organizations. He has served as a National Director of both the American Advertising Federation (AAF) and the Association of National Advertisers (ANA) and is presently on the board of the Advertising Council, Inc.

Chuck and his wife Sharon reside in Atlanta, USA.

Sally Hancock

Sally is Chief Executive of Redmandarin, a company which she co-founded in April 1999 and which has rapidly established itself at the forefront of international independent sponsorship thinking. The company has provided international and impartial strategic sponsorship solutions to a wide range of clients, including Unilever, Siemens, Barclays, T-Mobile, BT and PricewaterhouseCoopers.

Sally has led multiple strategic sponsorship consulting projects including the development of a global sponsorship framework for Unilever and a European non-sport sponsorship strategy for Visa International.

Prior to Redmandarin, Sally was Senior Vice President of Strategic Planning for Octagon Marketing, and also led the European consulting division of API before its merger with Advantage and absorption into Octagon. International strategic sponsorship consulting projects developed in that time included:

- The development of a first-time sponsorship strategy for Cereal Partners (a joint venture between General Mills and Nestlé), negotiation of the Official Product category for the 1998 World Cup in France and co-ordination of the sponsorship across 34 markets.
- Enhancement of Reebok's involvement in the UEFA Champions League.
- A feasibility study for Visa on the viability of sponsorship programmes in developing markets in Central Europe, Middle East and Africa.

Sally is a regular commentator on sponsorship issues on TV and in the media, and lives in London with her partner and two small children.

Adam Morgan

Adam Morgan is the founding partner of eatbigfish, an international brand consultancy specializing in challenger behaviour and strategy in today's business world. His early career was spent in advertising in the UK and US, where he became increasingly interested in the subject of challenger brands and in 1997 he established the Challenger Project. This continually evolving study led to the publication of *Eating The Big Fish: how Challenger Brands can compete against Market Leaders* which has been widely acclaimed as a marketing bible. Adam is also a popular speaker at business and marketing conferences around the world and is currently working on his next book.

Ravi Naidoo

Ravi is the founder and Managing Director of Interactive Africa (www.interactive.africa.com), a Cape Town based marketing and media company. He is an MBA graduate of the University of Cape Town and has focused on media and marketing subsequent to a detour from an academic career. Ravi has been involved in a number of significant projects and has been the mastermind behind a number of 'big ideas' including South

Africa's bid to host the 2010 World Cup Soccer and Mark Shuttleworth's 'First African in Space' project.

Sean O'Neill

Sean O'Neill is Brand and Market Communication Director for Diageo plc, the world's leading premium alcoholic drinks company. He has global responsibility for the development of non-advertising communication strategies across the company's priority brands, which include Guinness, Johnnie Walker, Smirnoff, Baileys, J&B, Tanqueray, Captain Morgan, Gordon's, and Jose Cuervo Tequila.

Before this, from 1996 to 2001, Sean was Global Communication Director for the Guinness company prior to the merger with its sister company UDV, the world's largest spirits company. In this role he had functional responsibility across the various communication disciplines including corporate, brand and internal communication as well as corporate citizenship.

Sean joined Guinness from Burson-Marsteller, one of the world's largest communication consultancies. In his seven years with the company, he worked in London, Russia, Egypt and Australia performing a variety of roles including General Manager of the company's Middle East business, Communication Director for the British government funded privatization of industry in Russia and running corporate and marketing communication across Asia for some of the company's leading clients.

He is a graduate in History from the University of London.

Michael Payne

Michael Payne, as Marketing Director for the IOC, is responsible for co-ordinating and directing the Olympic Movement's marketing programmes. The portfolio ranges from overseeing all revenue generating programmes including broadcast rights, global and local sponsorship programmes, licensing and Games ticketing programmes through to the overall 'brand' management and international promotion of the Olympic Movement with such programmes as the 'Celebrate Humanity' campaign.

Michael first began working for the Olympic Movement in 1983, as the Project Director for the IOC's then marketing agency, responsible for developing a global marketing strategy for the Olympic Movement, which subsequently led to the launch of the TOP Programme in 1985. In 1988, Michael was invited to join the IOC as the organization's first Marketing Director, and establish an in-house marketing department. Since 1988, Michael has led the IOC's overall marketing operations – directing marketing programmes for six Winter Olympic Games, and six Summer Olympic Games, currently working on Salt Lake 2002, Athens 2004, Torino 2006 and Beijing 2008.

Prior to joining the IOC, Michael had spent a number of years helping to develop marketing programmes for a cross-section of international sports events, including the first World Athletics Championships in 1983, the English Test Match Cricket Series through to the launch of the first London Marathon. In the mid-70s. Michael competed on the international ski circuit as a member of the British team, twice becoming British Professional Freestyle Ski Champion.

A British citizen, born in London 1958, married with a young family (two sons and a daughter aged 7, 5 and 3), he now lives in Lausanne, Switzerland.

Harlan Stone

Harlan recently joined Velocity Sports & Entertainment as a Principal. Harlan will spearhead Velocity's efforts in marketing and promotional areas related to television packaging, and property and event consulting.

Prior to joining Velocity, Harlan was CEO of Momentum Worldwide, a division of McCann-Erickson World Group, one of the world's largest marketing communications companies. Harlan was responsible for a 1,600-person global promotional/event marketing agency and fuelled revenue growth to approximately $200 million. Prior to Momentum, Harlan spent 14 years at Advantage International (renamed Octagon in 1998), where he spearheaded the dramatic domestic growth of that company from an

11-person agency with $1.5 million in revenue to a 175-person agency with $20 million in revenue.

Harlan also has a strong history with entrepreneurial enterprises, including his own sports marketing shop, Stone Sports, which was acquired by the New York Times Co. in 1985. In 2000, he was hired as CEO of internet start-up mysportsguru.com and just prior to moving to Momentum, he successfully negotiated mysportsguru.com's sale to myteam.com during the internet shakeout of 2000.

Harlan holds a B.A. in Political Science from the University of Virginia in Charlottesville, VA and lives with his wife Susan and their three children in Darien, CT.

Christopher D. Weil

With over 12 years' experience, Chris is one of the architects of the experiential branding vision. He has developed innovative sports and event marketing initiatives involving NASCAR, PGA, Ryder Cup, Tennis and the Olympics, and managed sponsorship and event programmes for Hyatt Hotels, Pepsi Cola and Gateway Computers.

Chris has been with Momentum for 5 years. As President of Momentum New York, Chris led the American Express global account team. He created a unique experiential marketing strategy for the brand, including initiatives embracing Disney, US Open, Tiger Woods and Madison Square Gardens.

Chris also conceived, developed and executed the Sheryl Crow and Friends concert in New York's Central Park for the launch of Blue from American Express – which won Momentum the marketing excellence award, the Super Reggie. He followed that success with another free concert in Central Park, this time for the introduction of the consumer electronics giant Best Buy to the New York marketplace – headliner Sting called the show one of the highlights of his career.

As Regional Director for Europe, Middle East and Africa, Chris restructured the offices and service offering improving the quality of Momentum's 33-office European network. He spearheaded the development of further pan-regional clients such as Interbrew, JTI and American Express.

He now moves back to New York as Chairman and Chief Executive, where he will head Momentum Worldwide with a mission to unify the world's leading experiential marketing agency, accelerate growth and increase collaborative efforts across the board with McCann Erickson WorldGroup clients.

Index